Tabitha L Barnett's

Majestic Mandalas

Volume 3

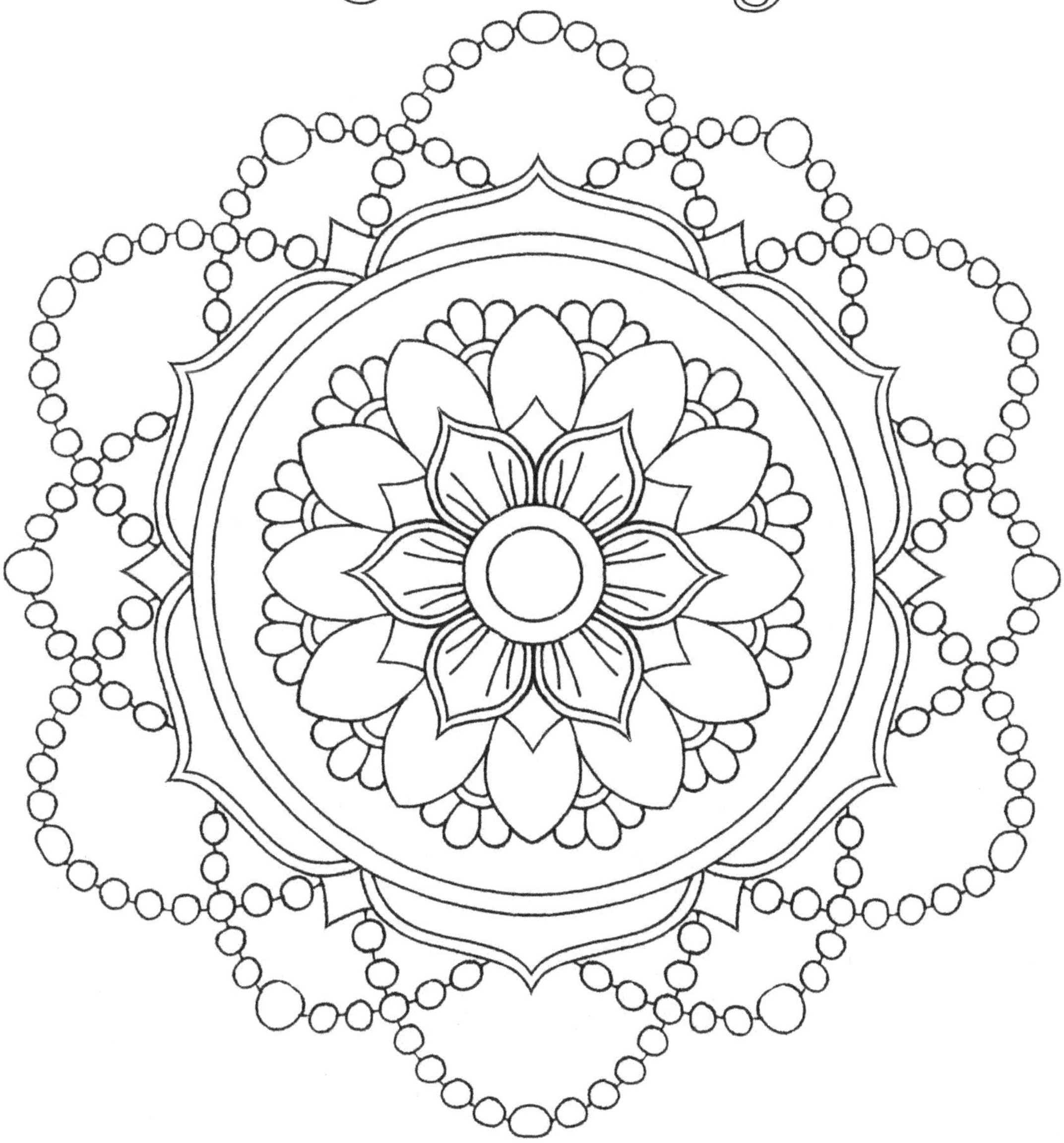

 facebook.com/tabbystangledart

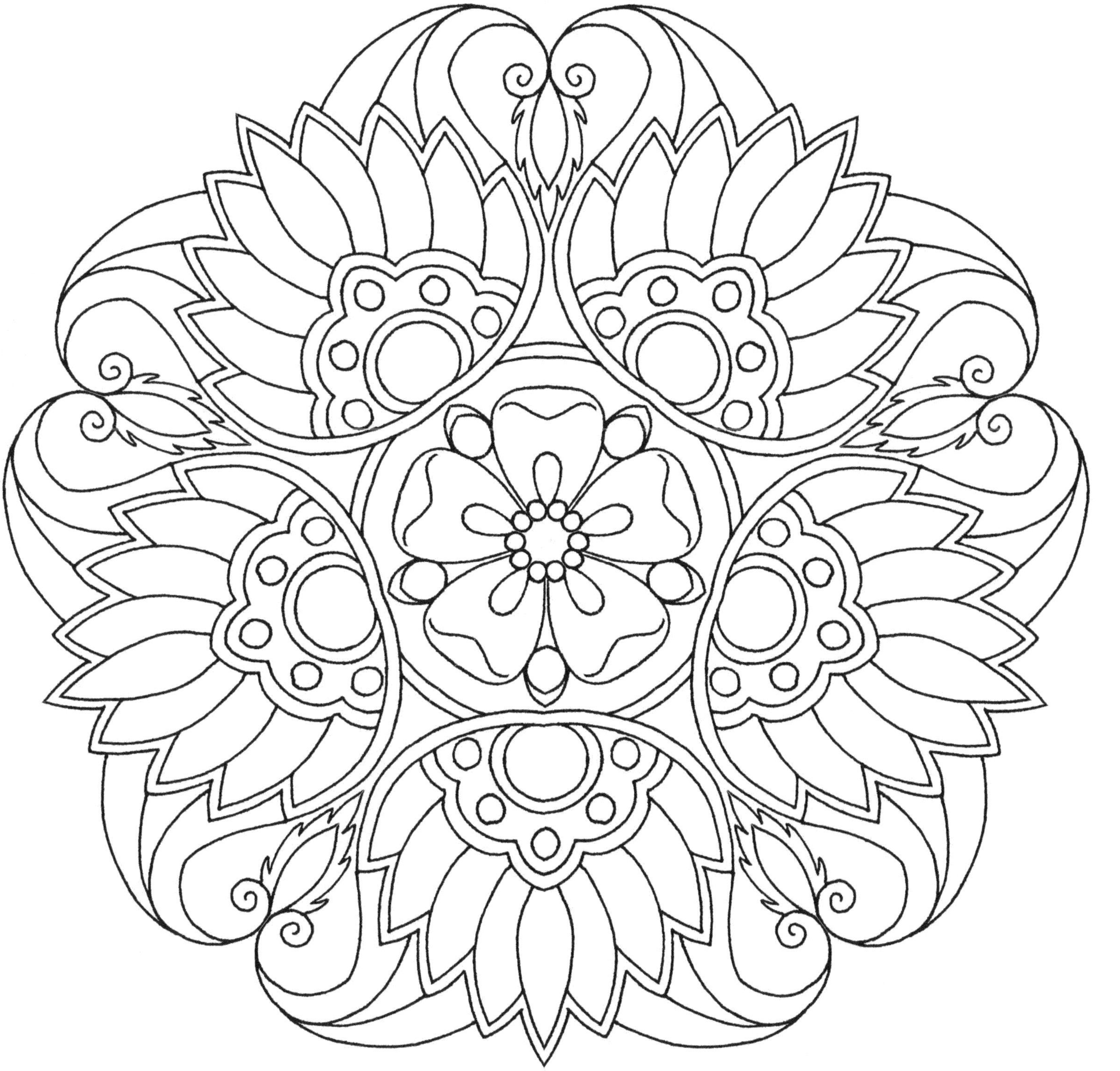

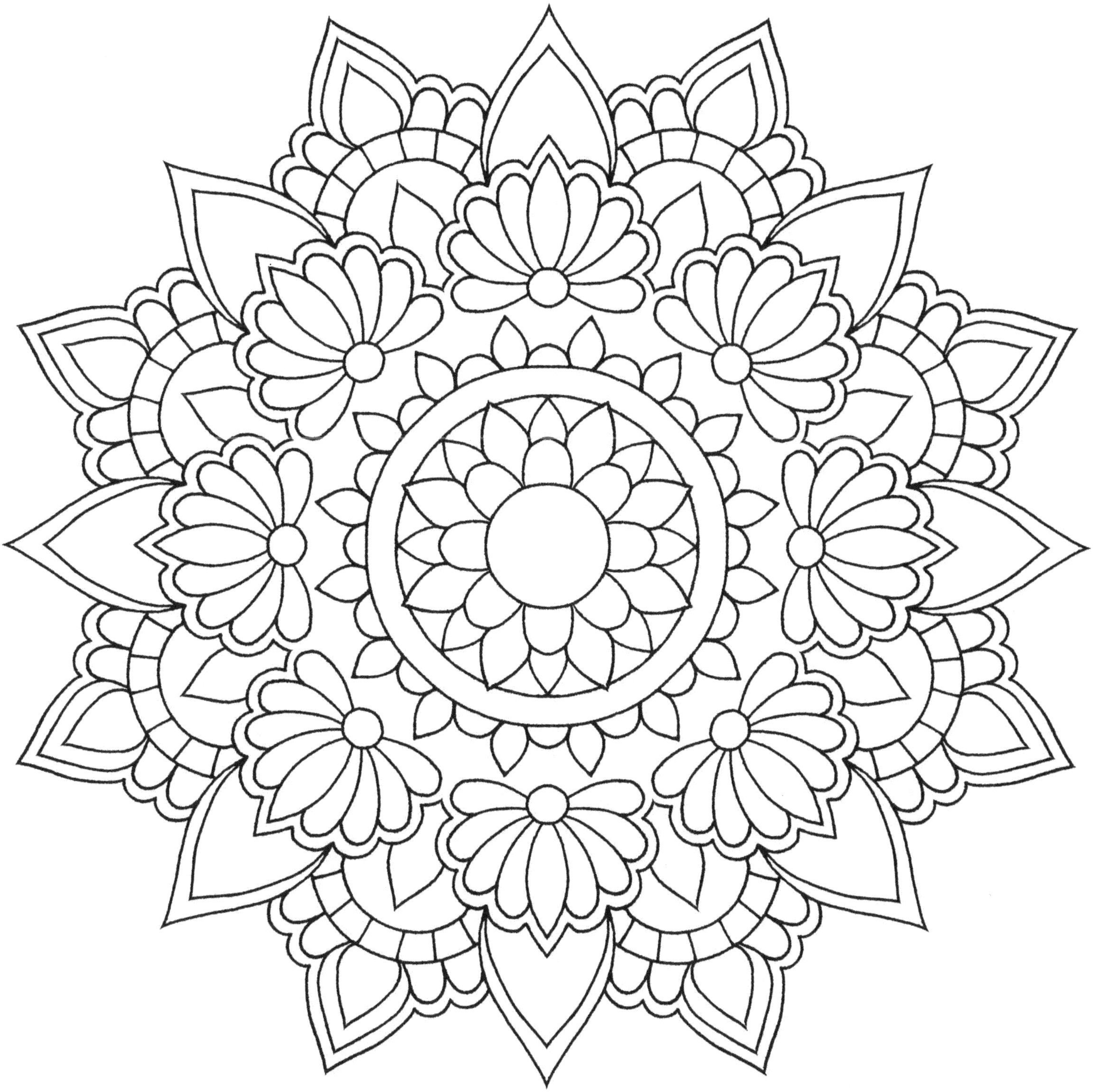

 facebook.com/tabbystangledart

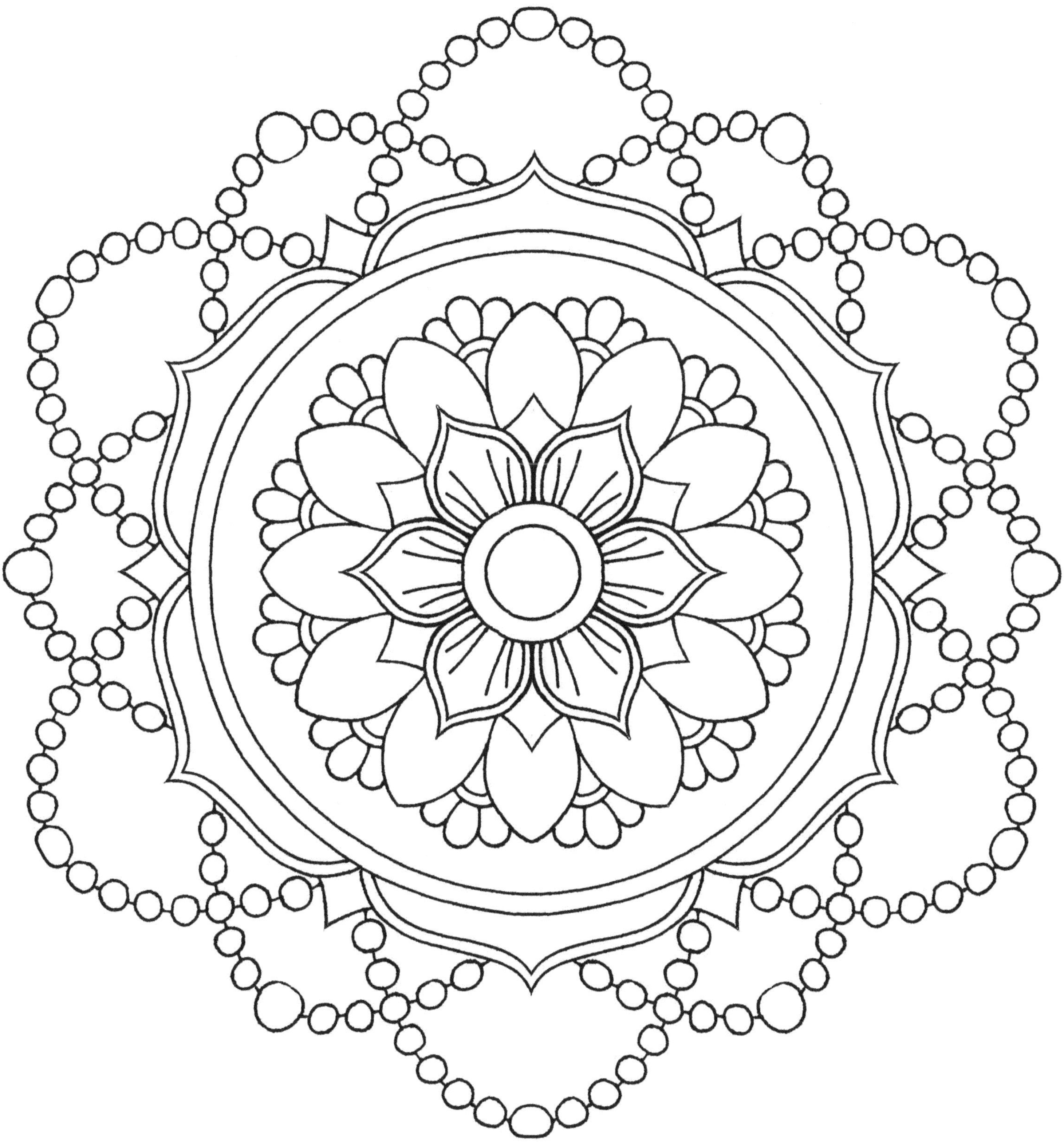

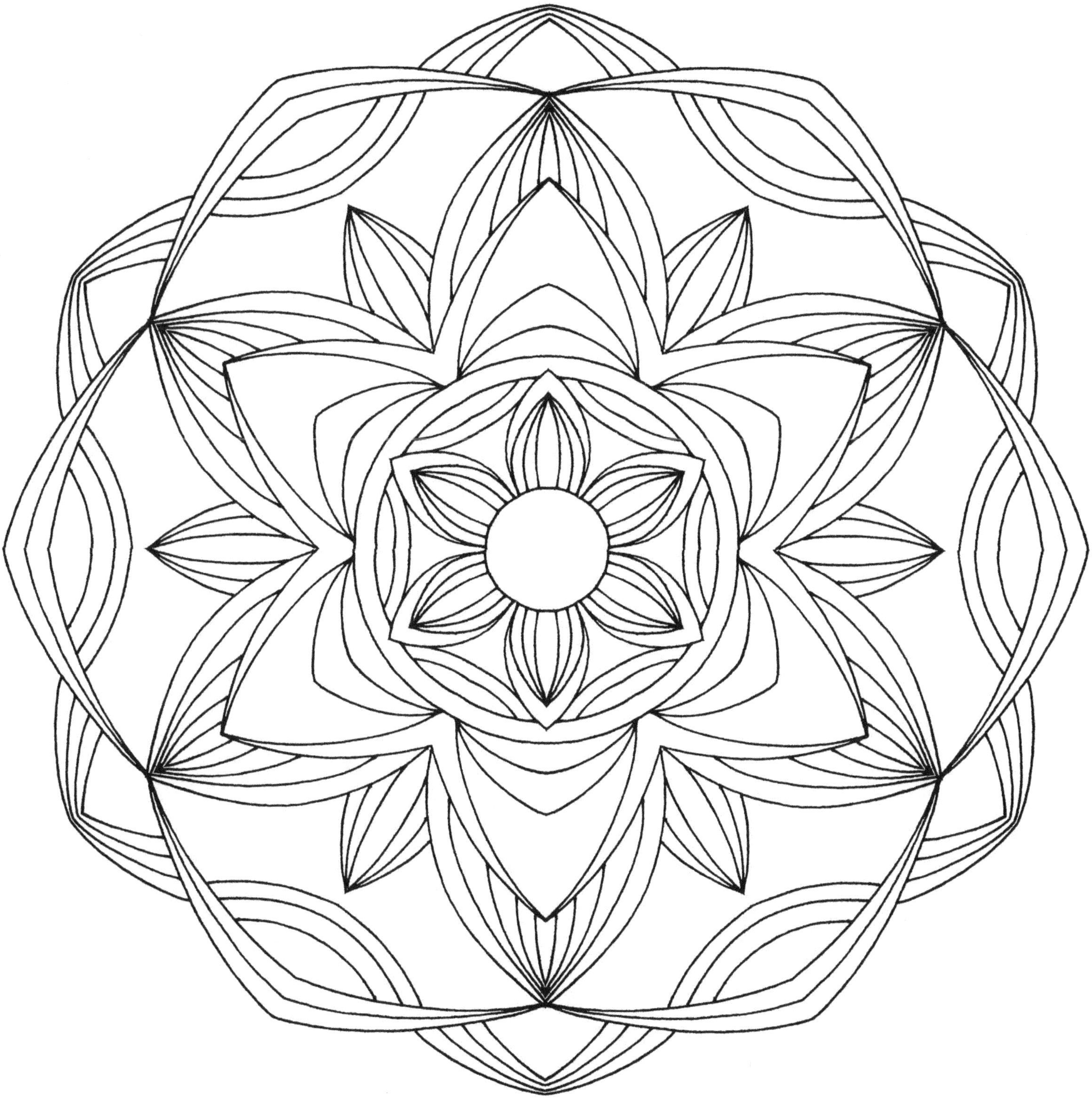

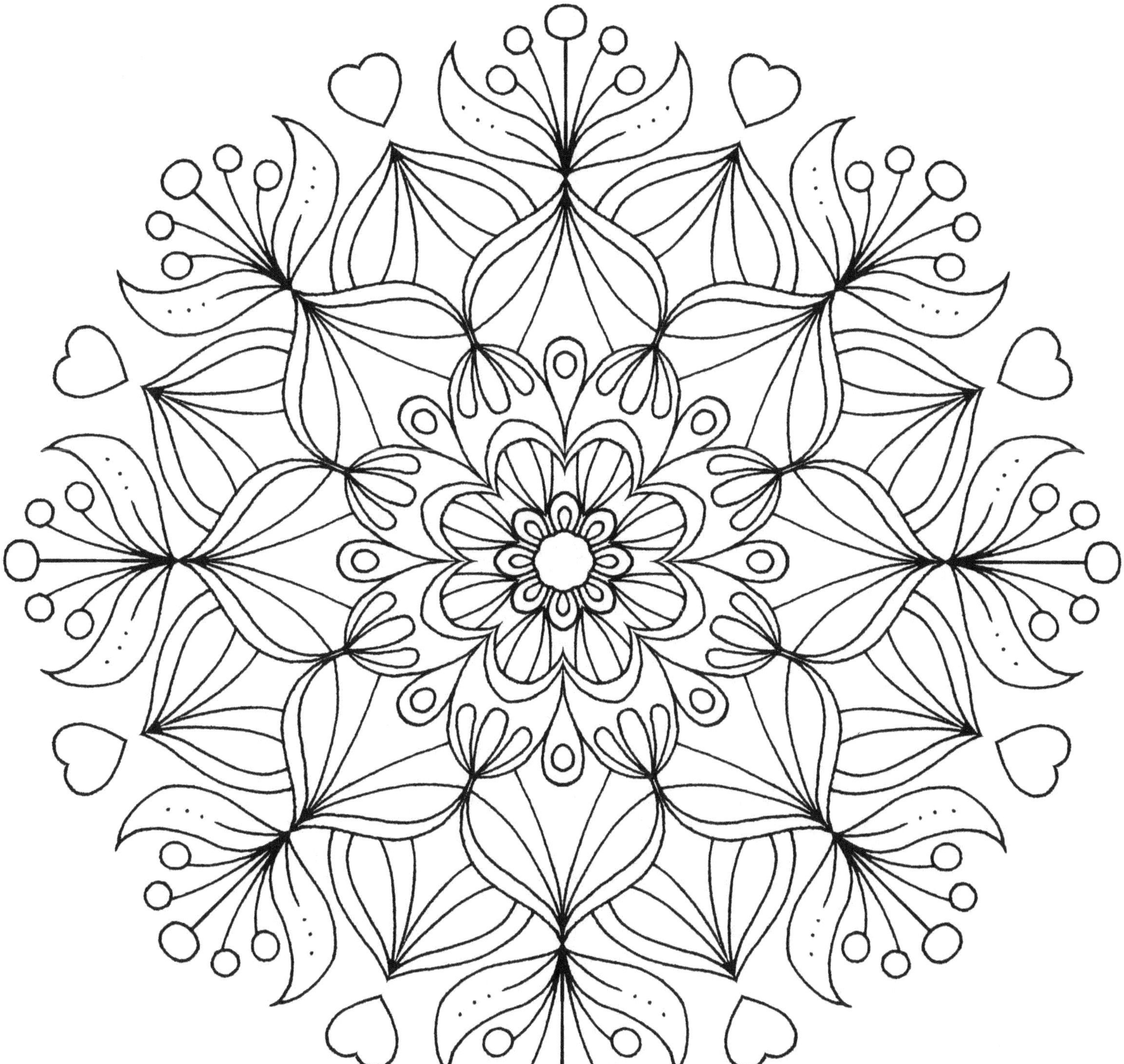

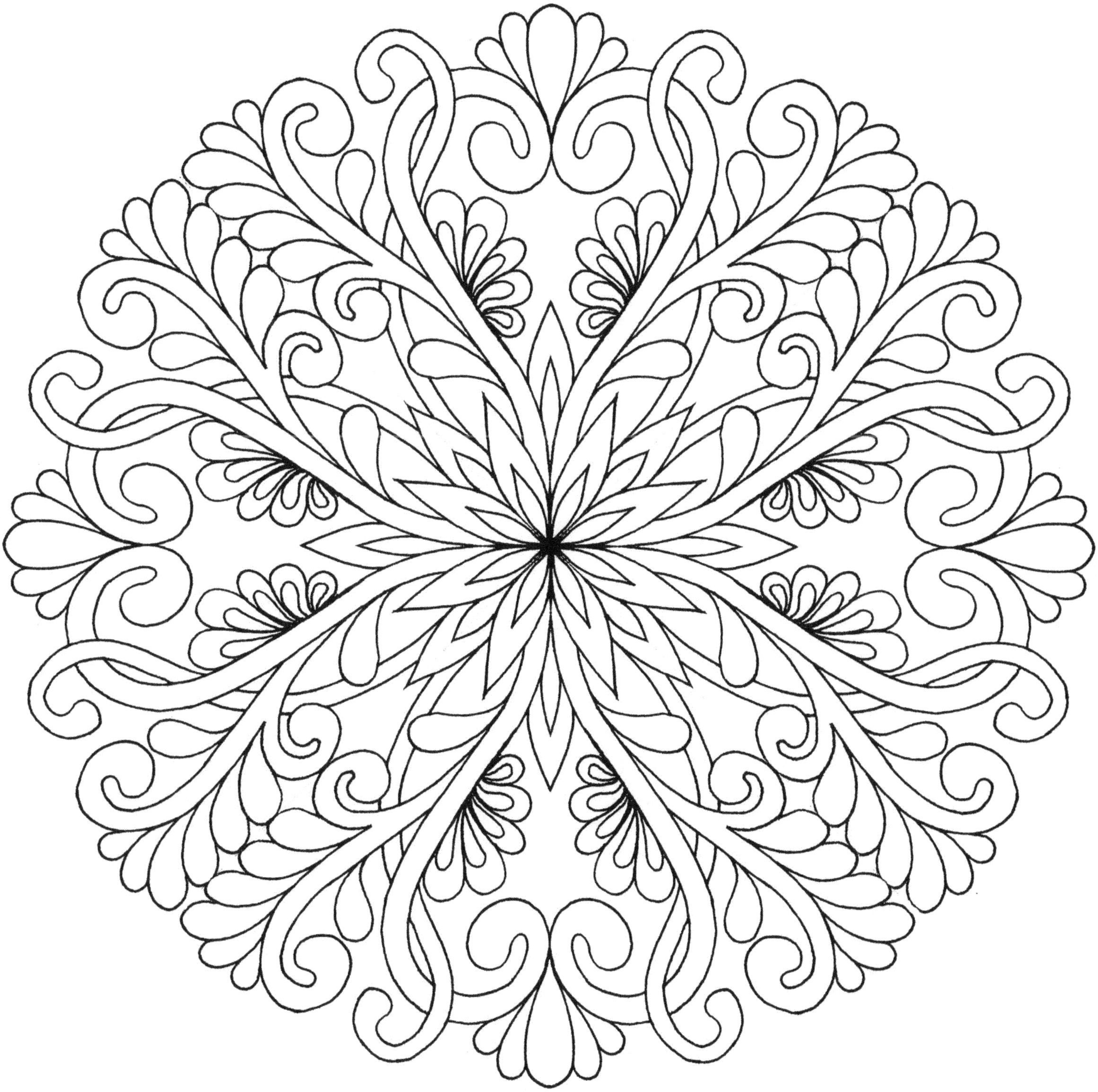

 facebook.com/tabbystangledart

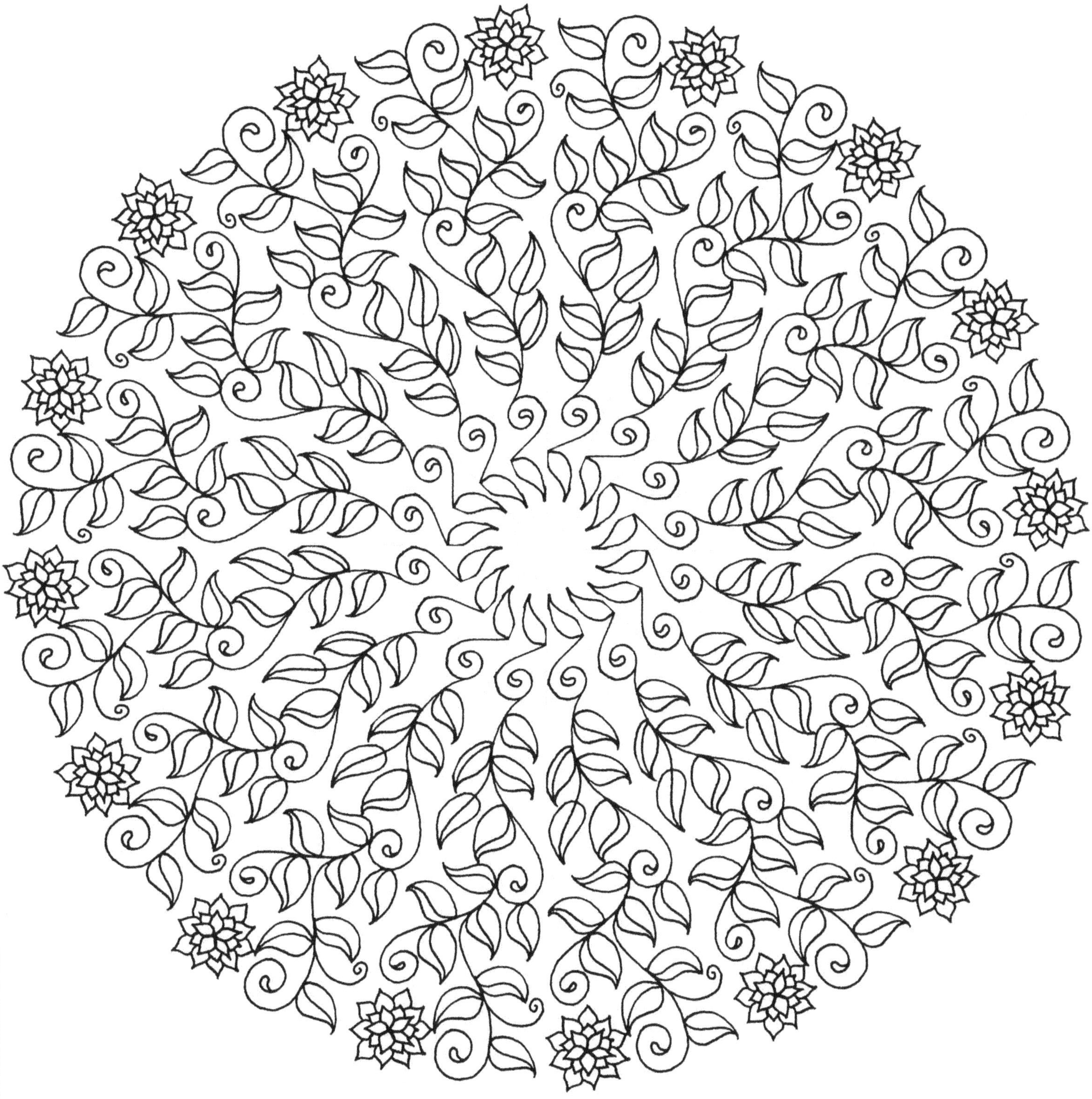

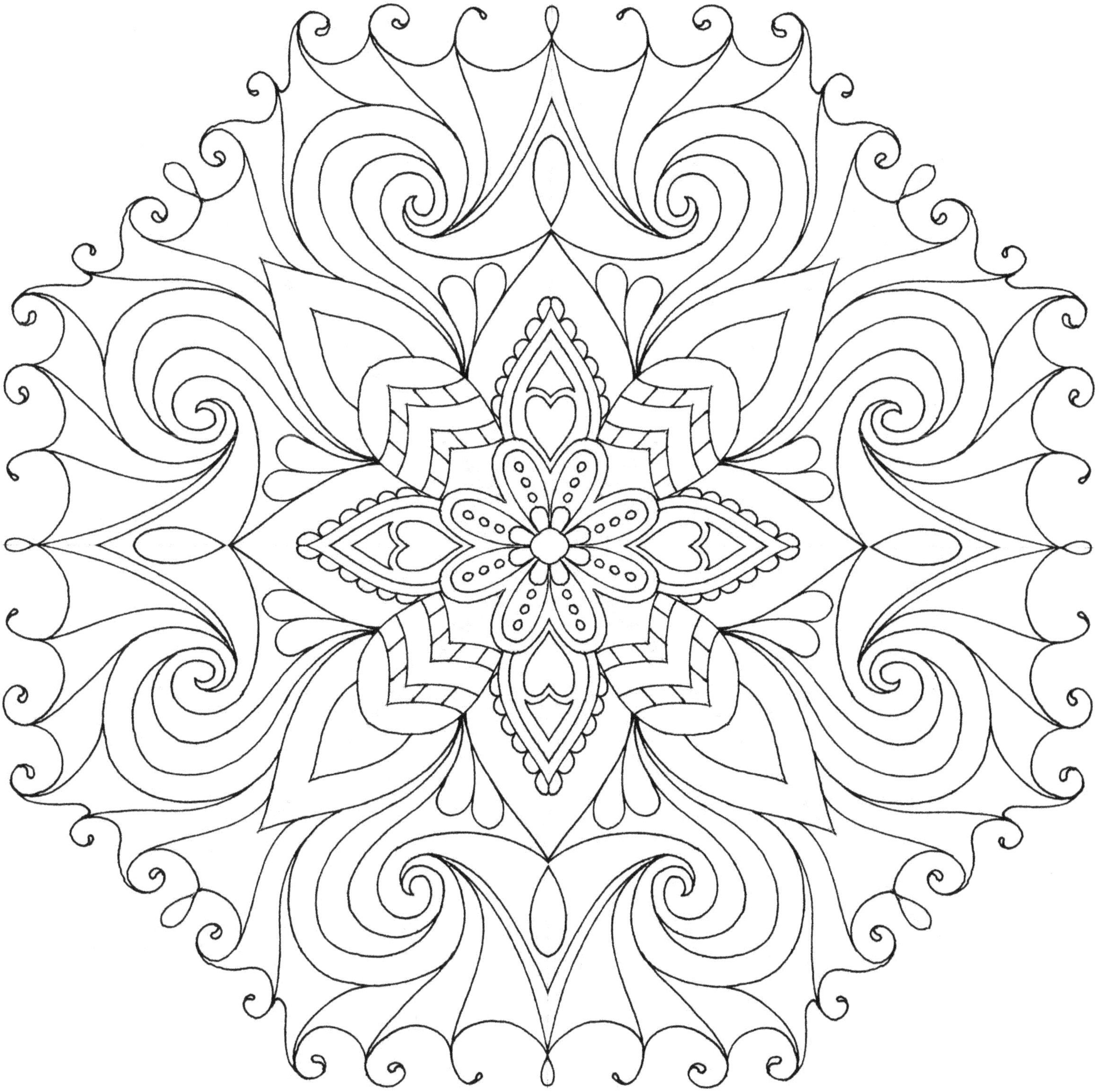

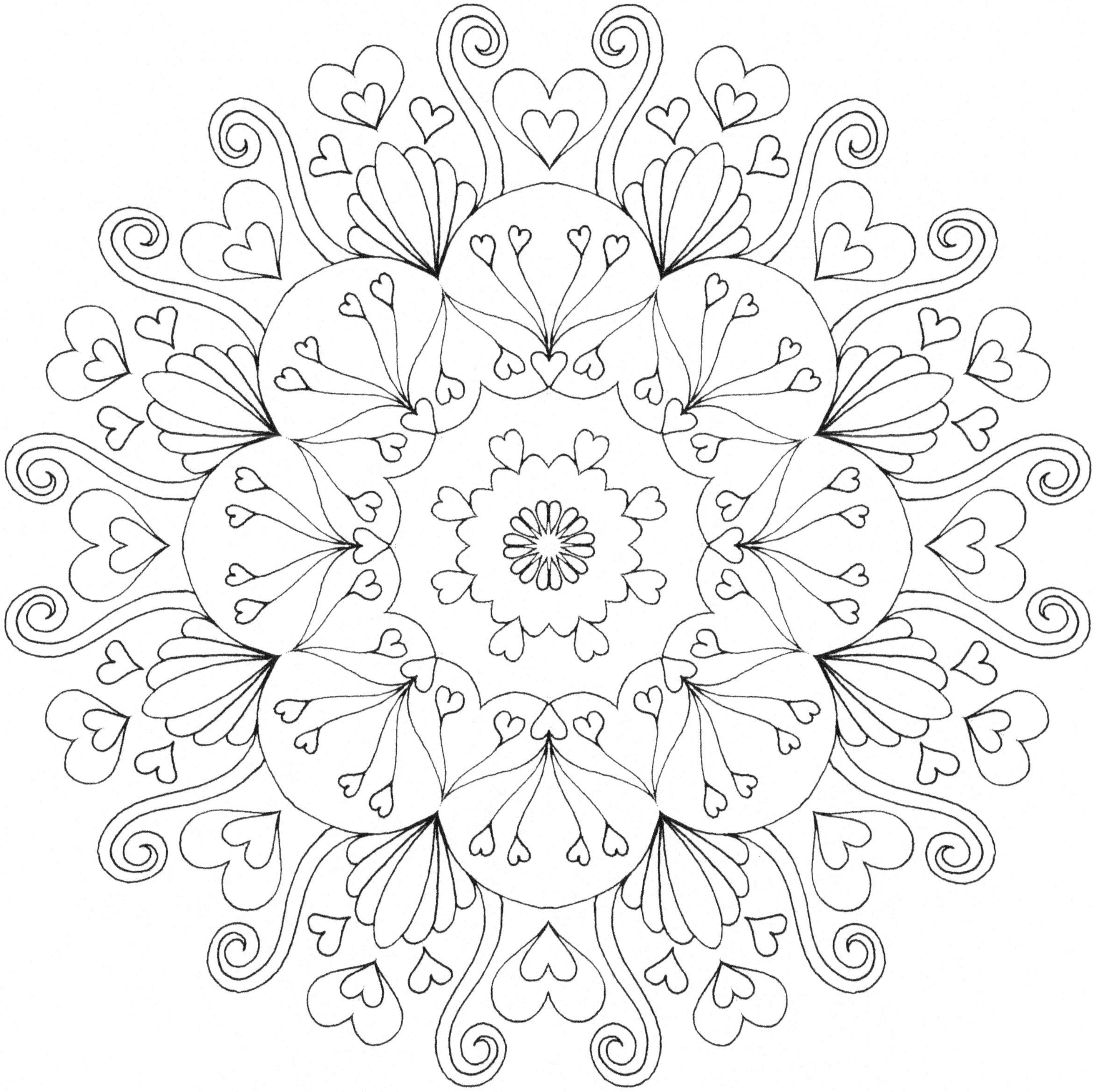

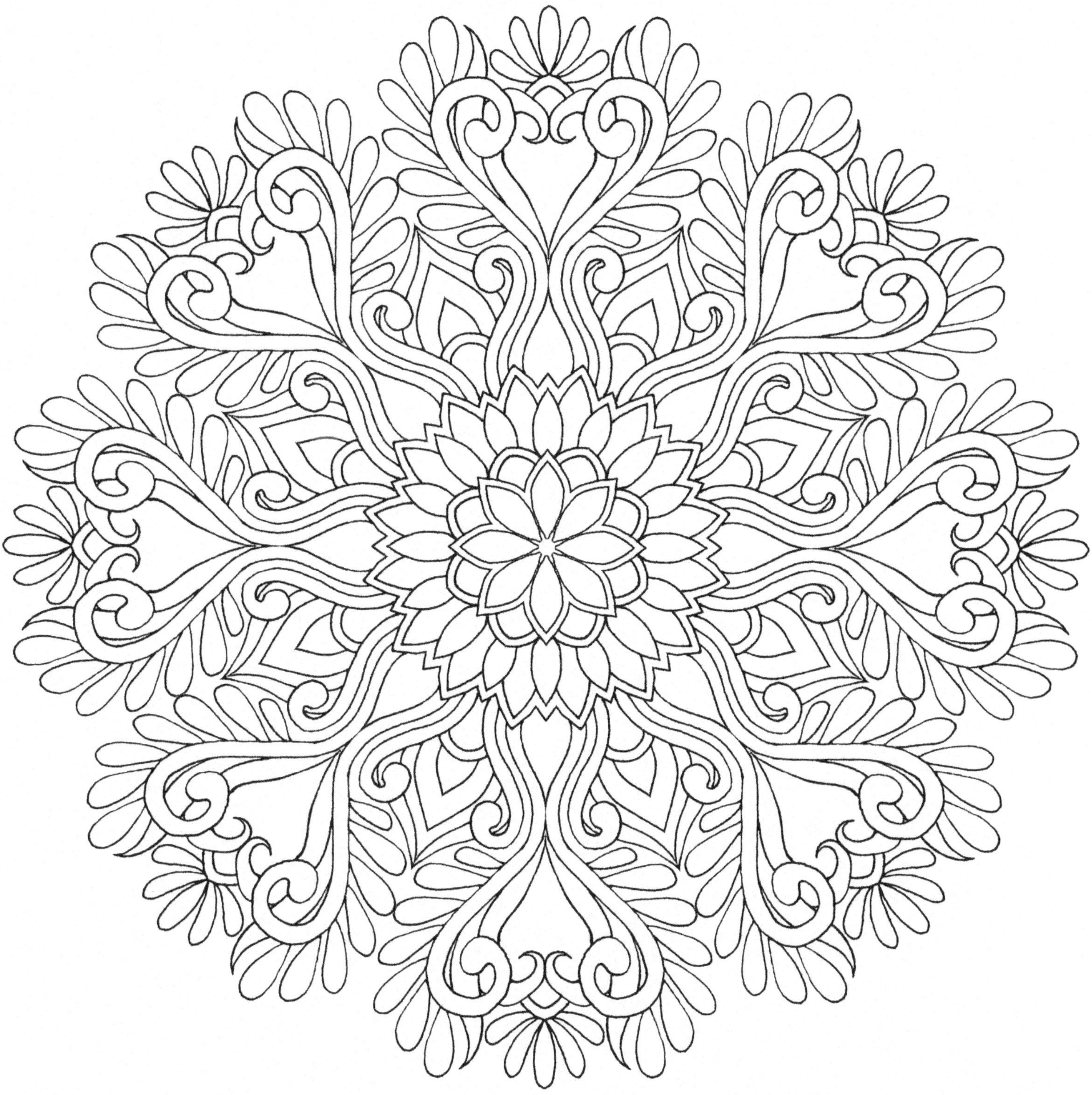

 facebook.com/tabbystangledart

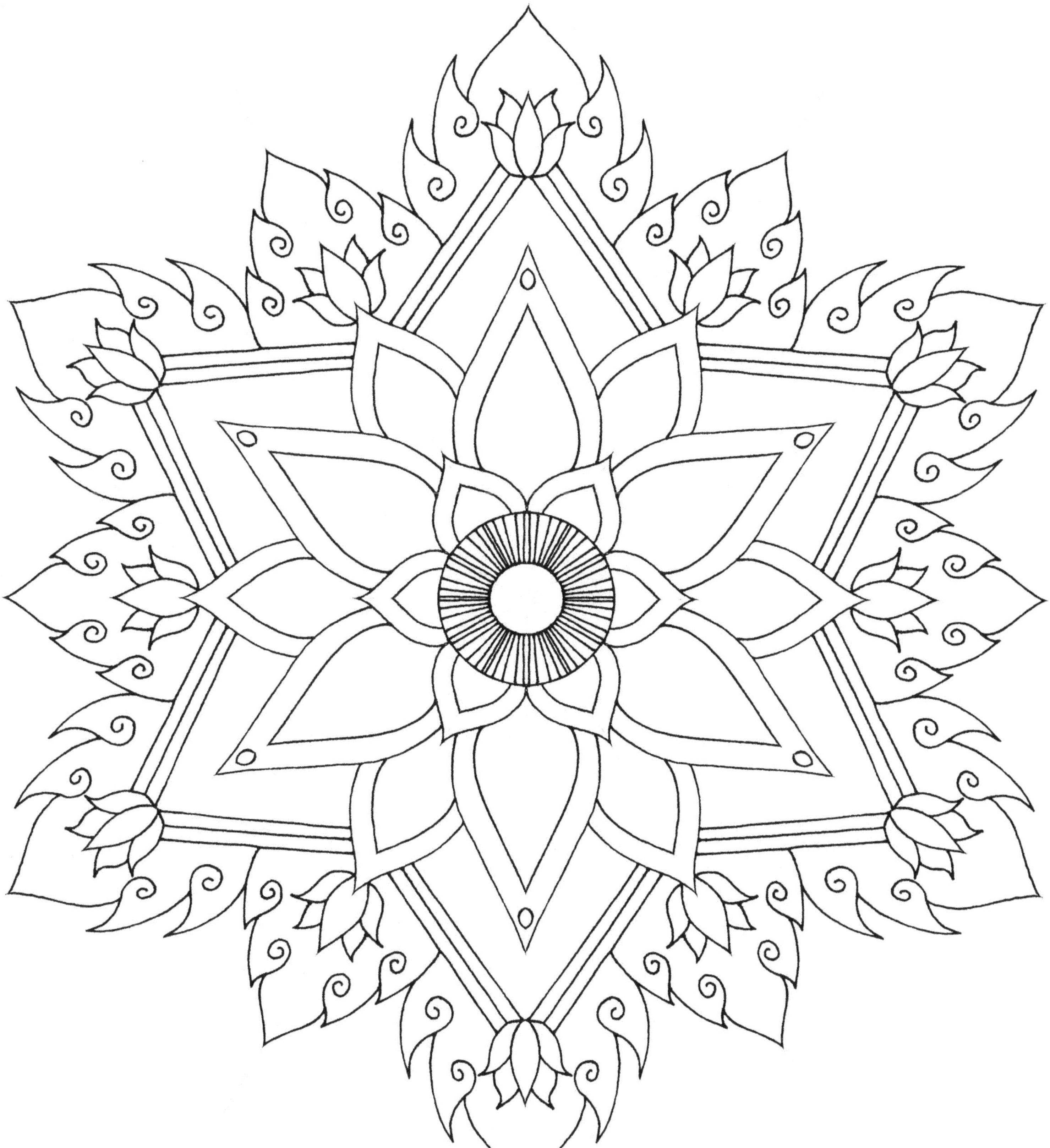

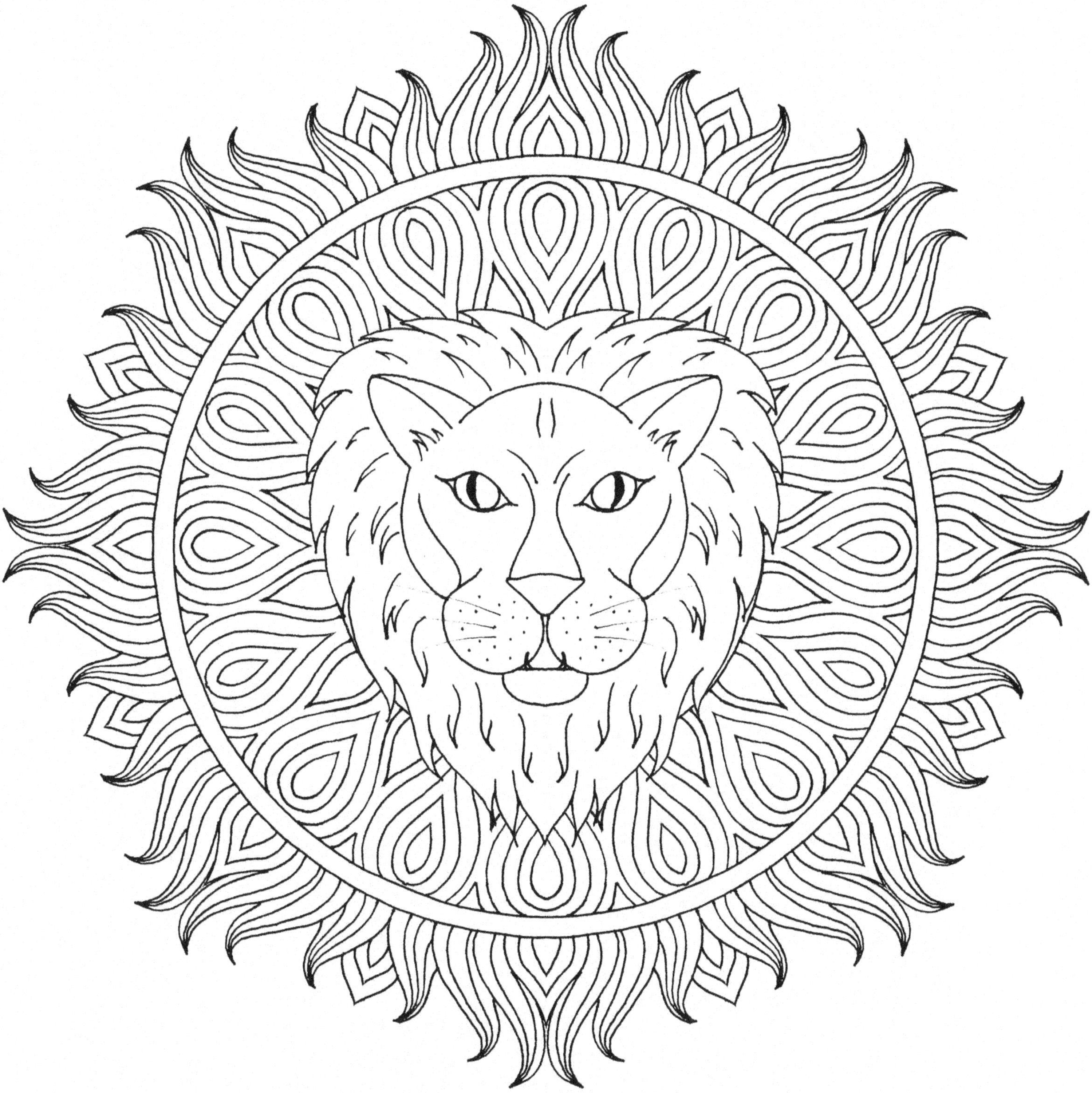

 facebook.com/tabbystangledart

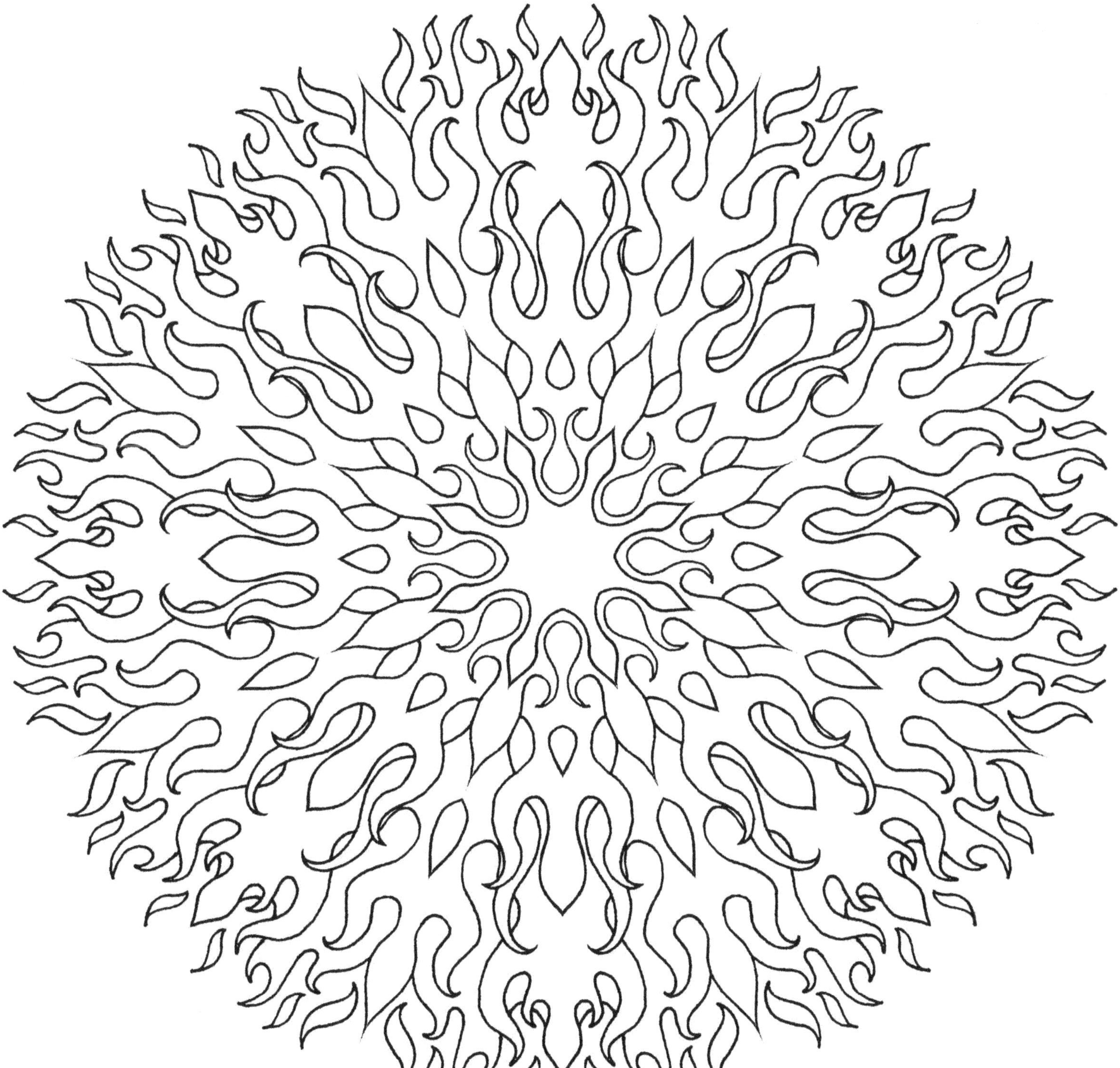

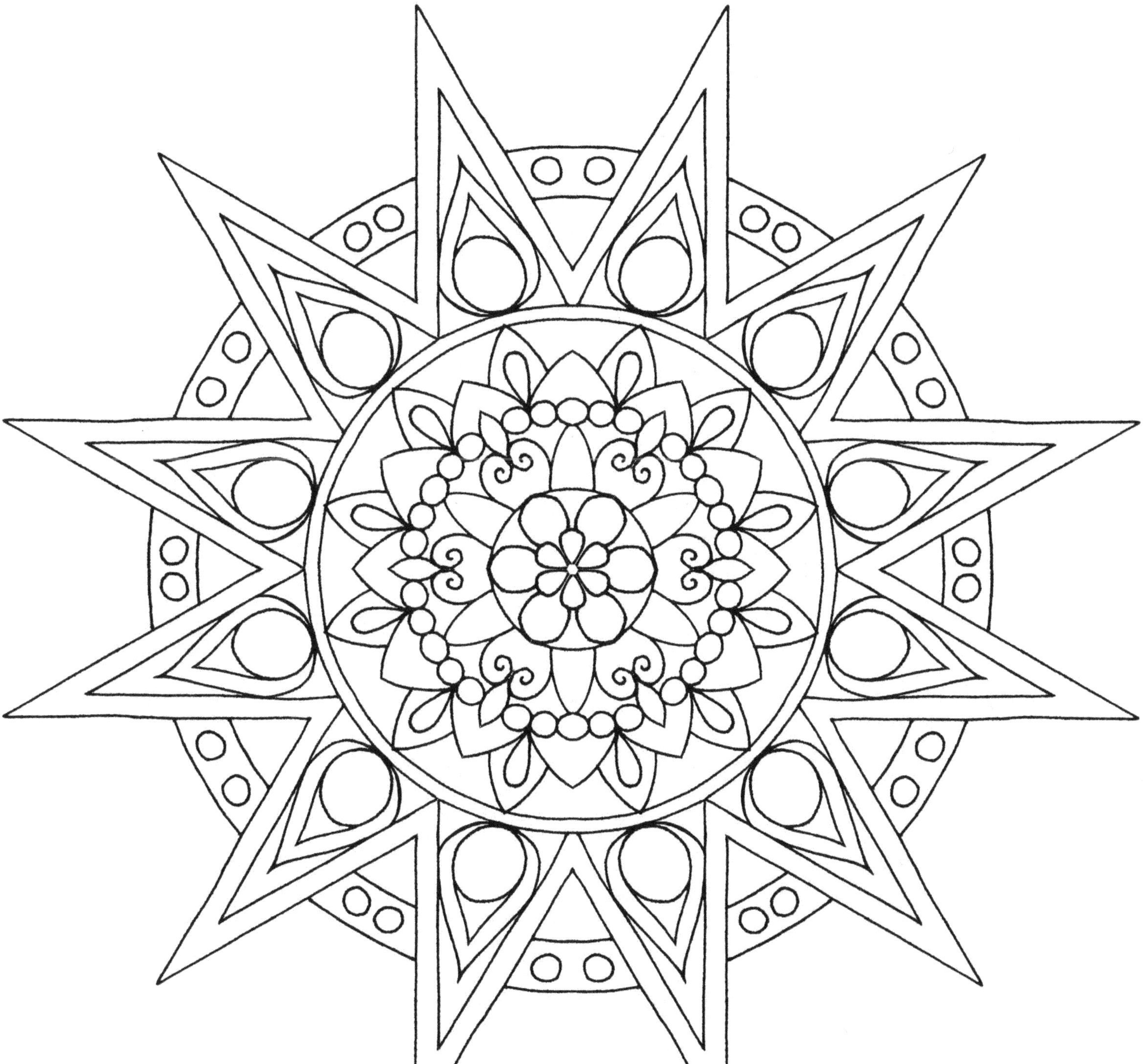

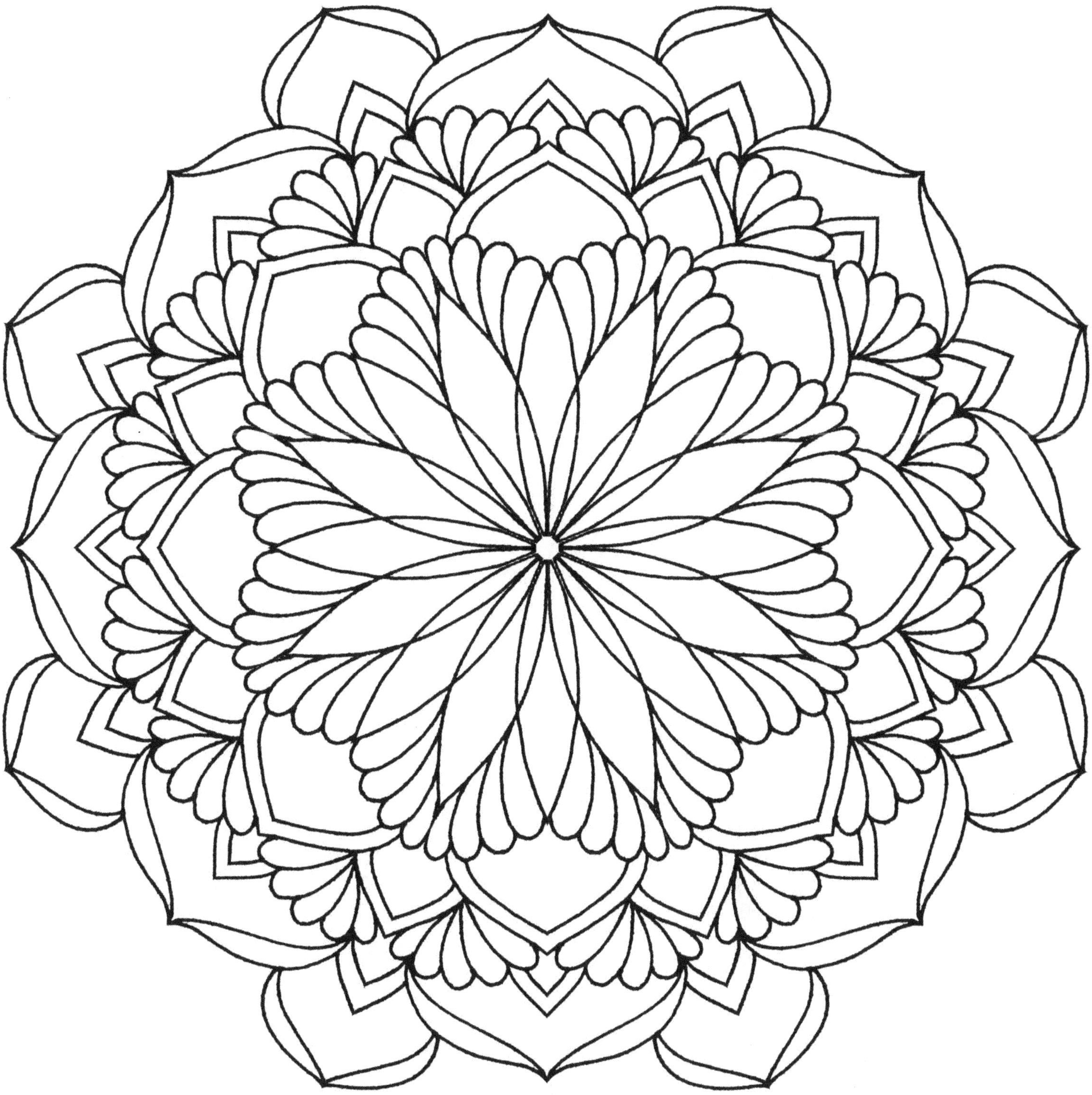

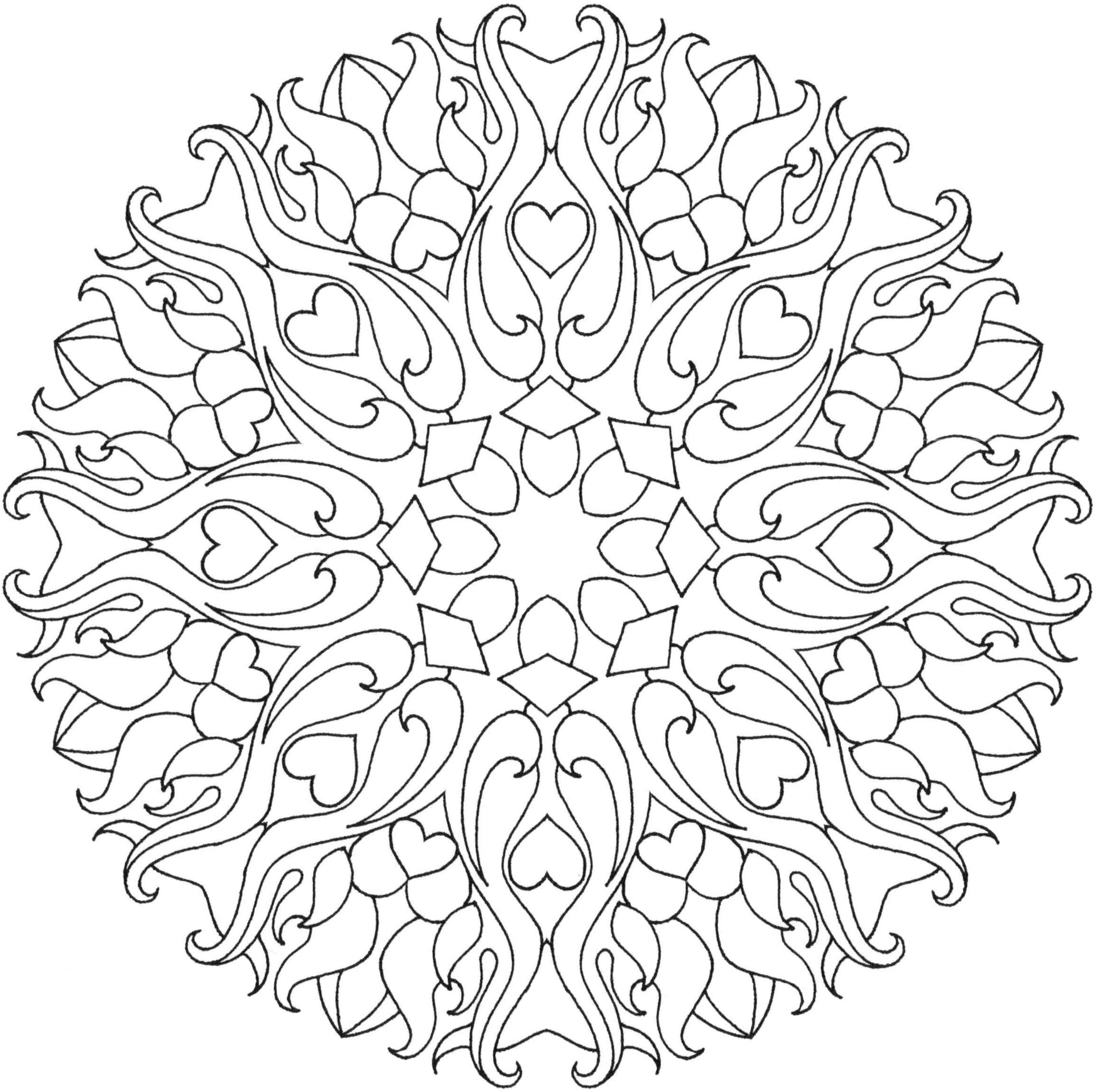

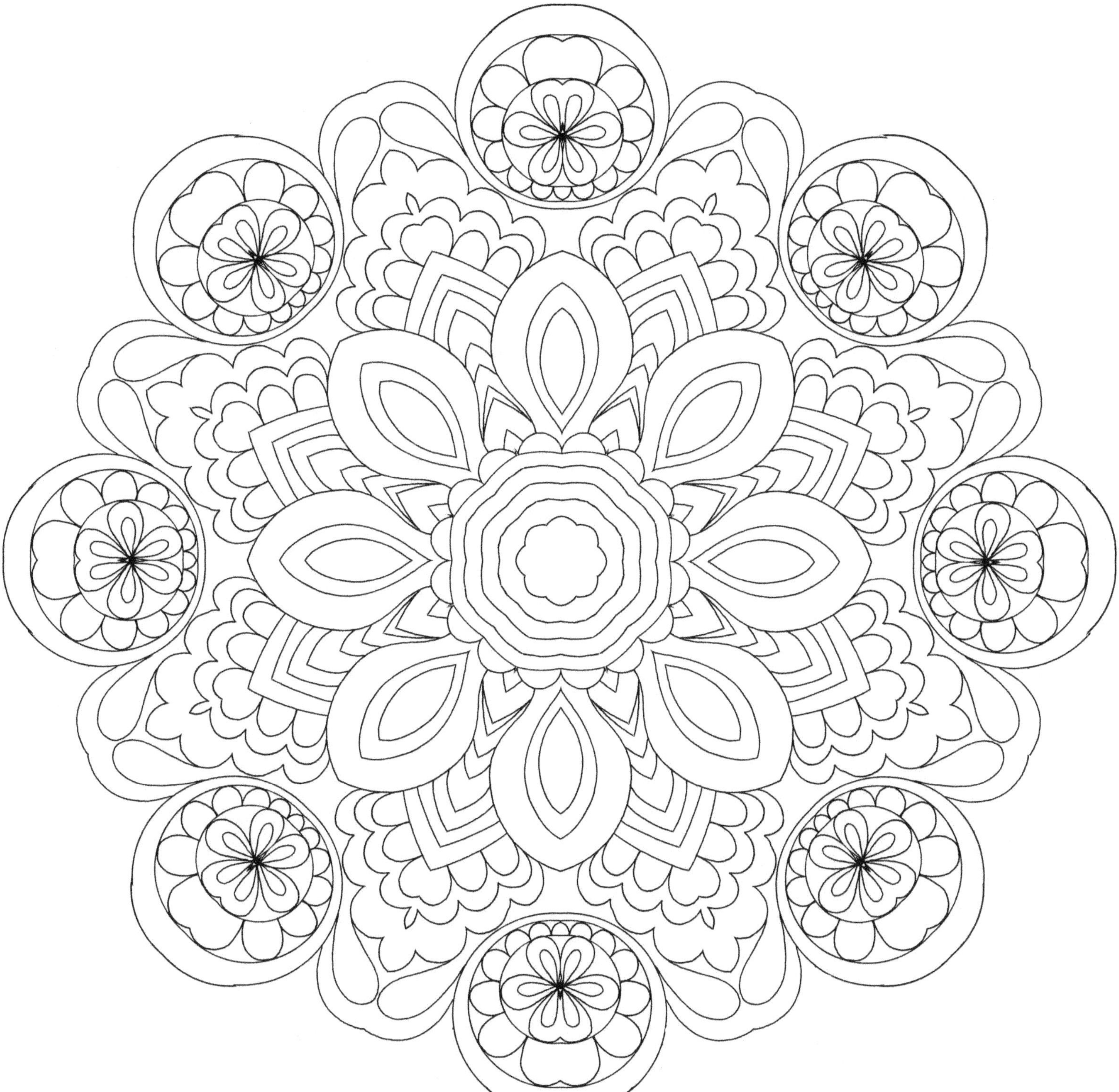

 facebook.com/tabbystangledart

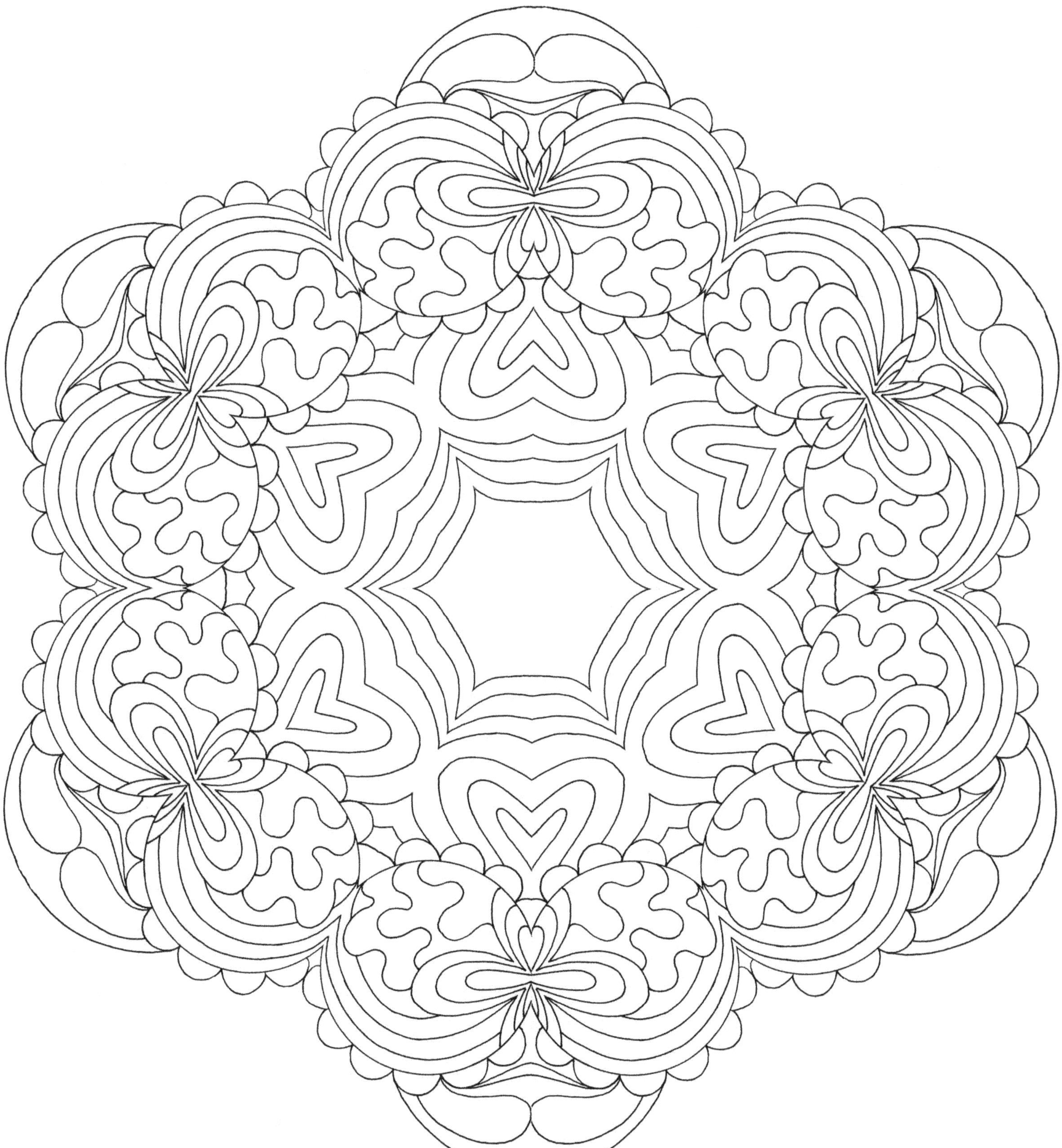

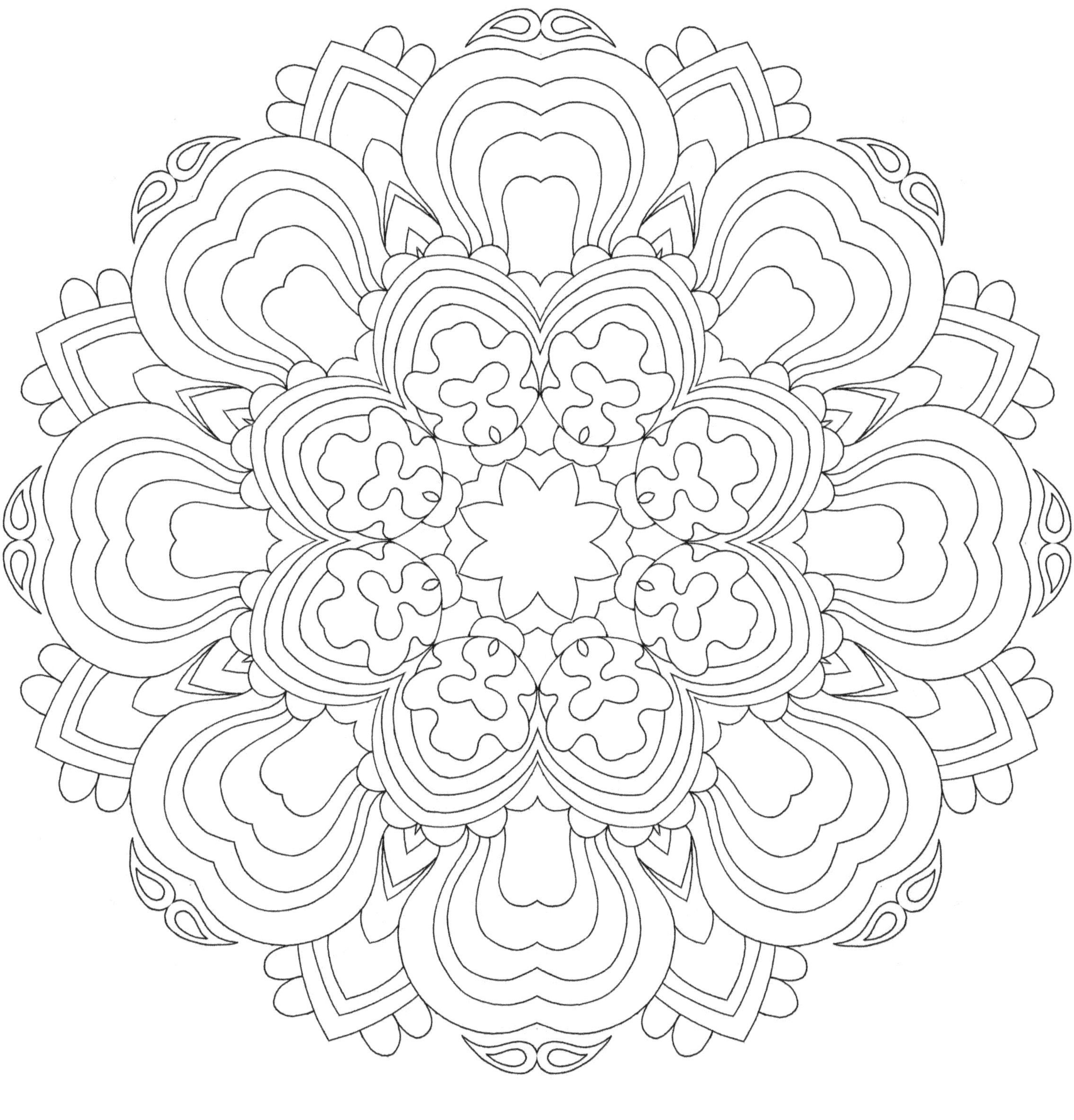

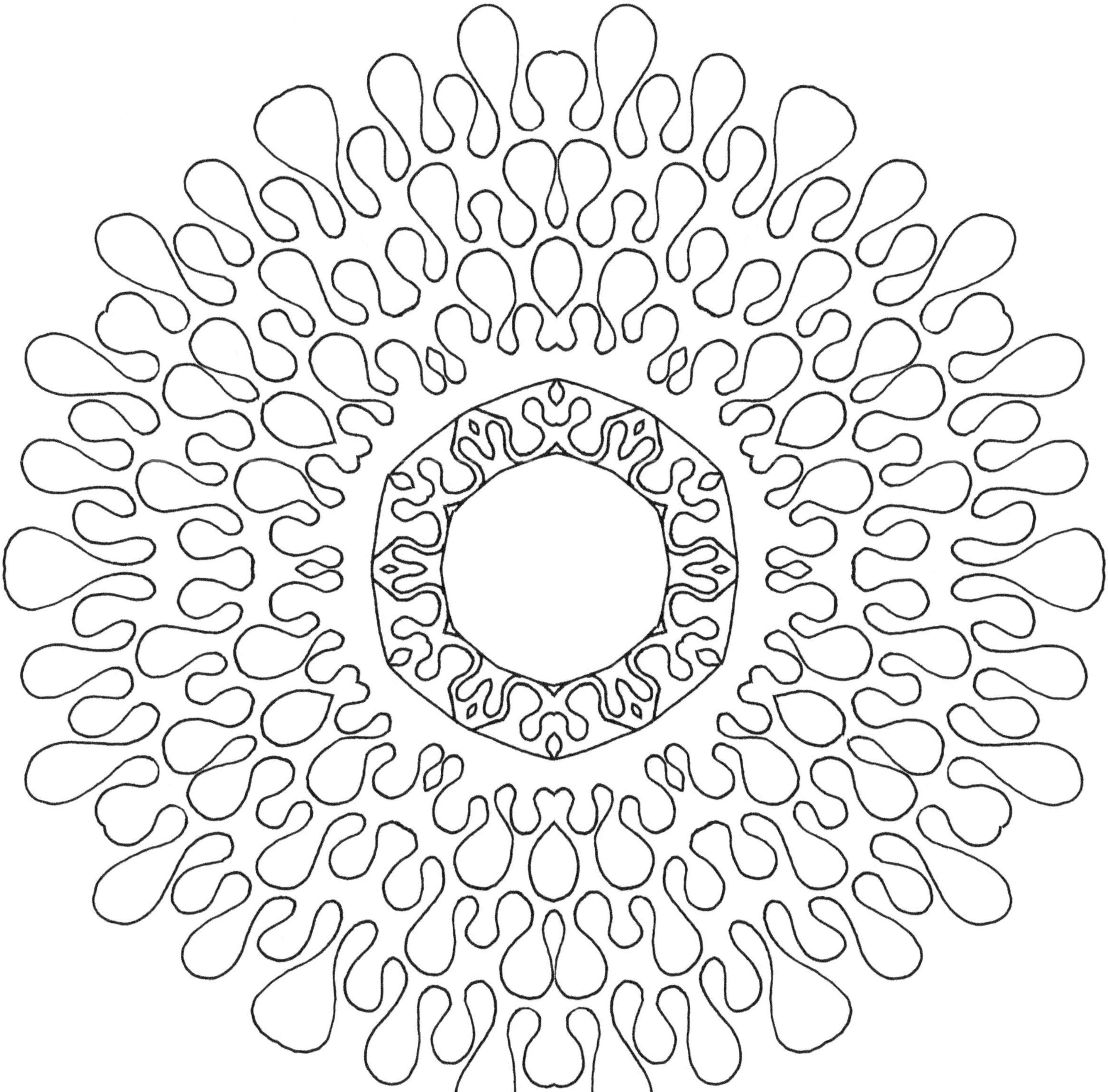

 facebook.com/tabbystangledart

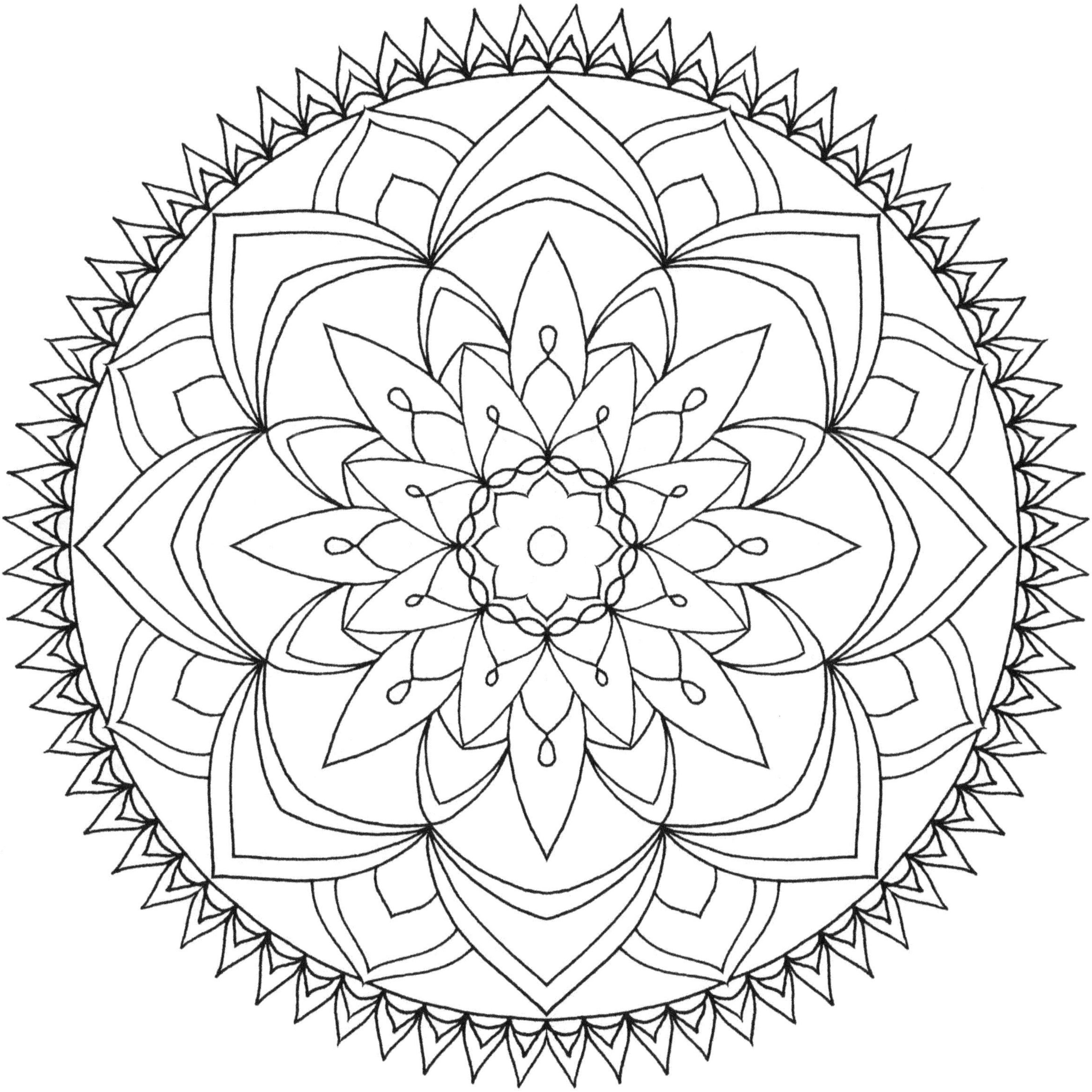

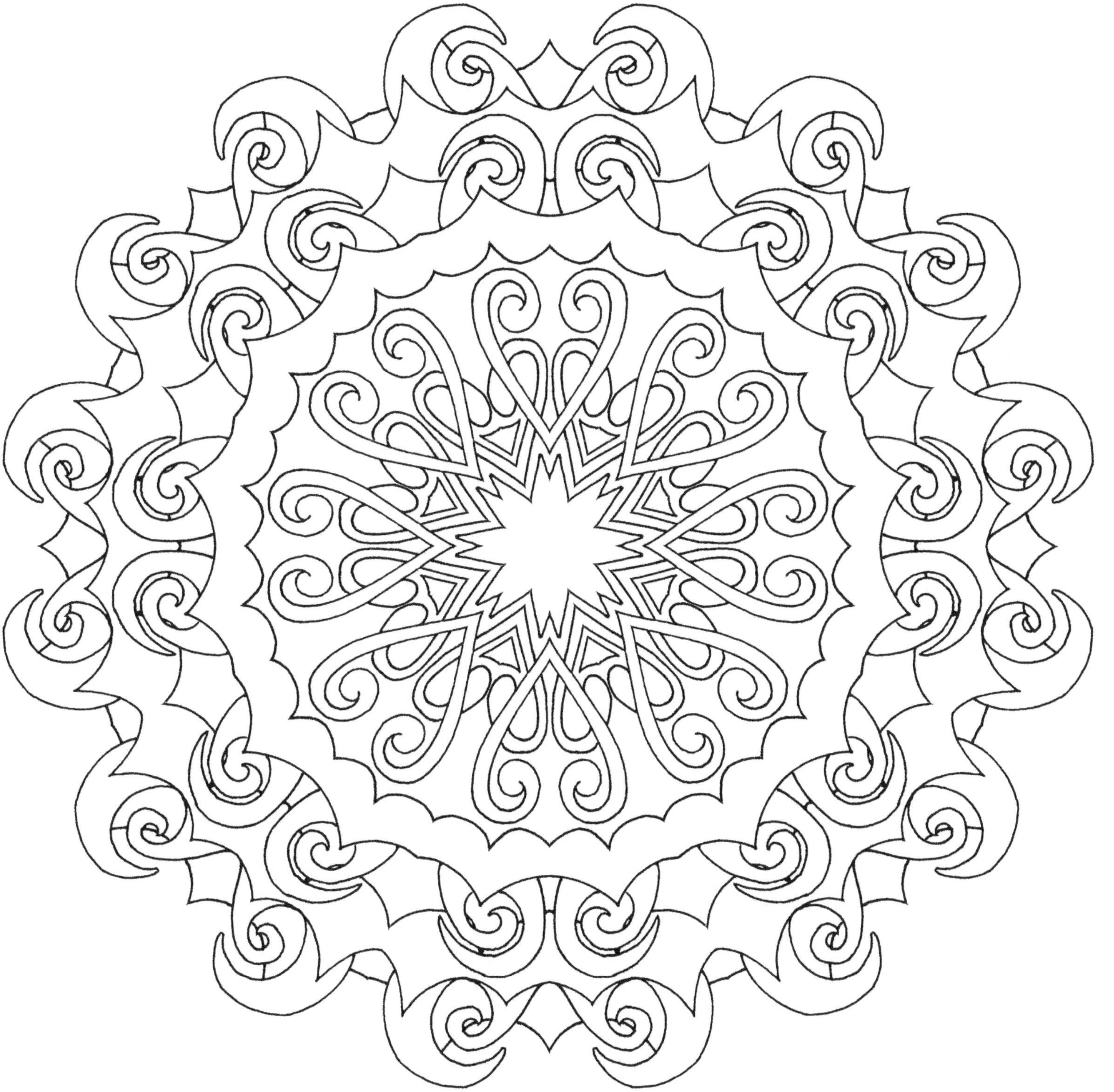

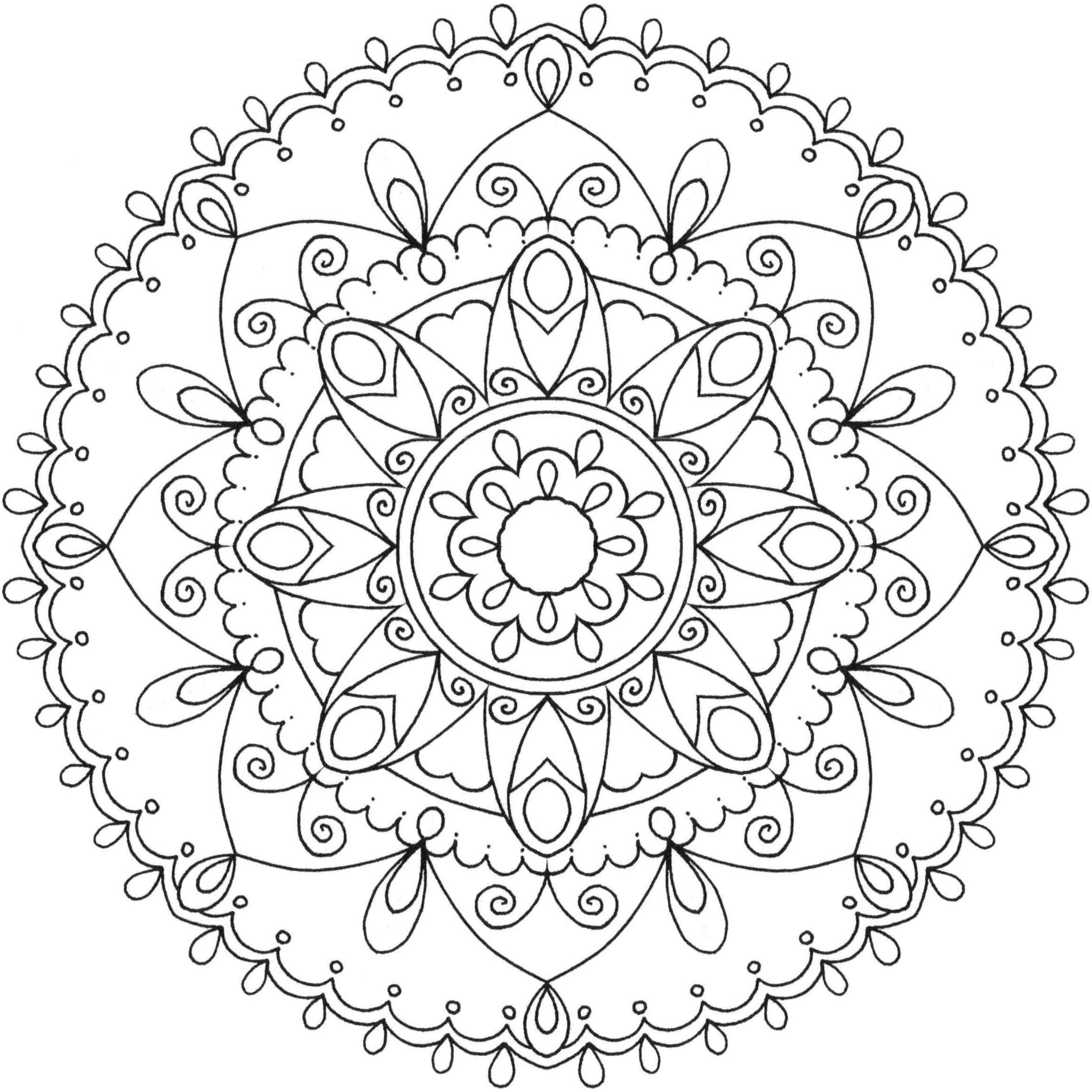

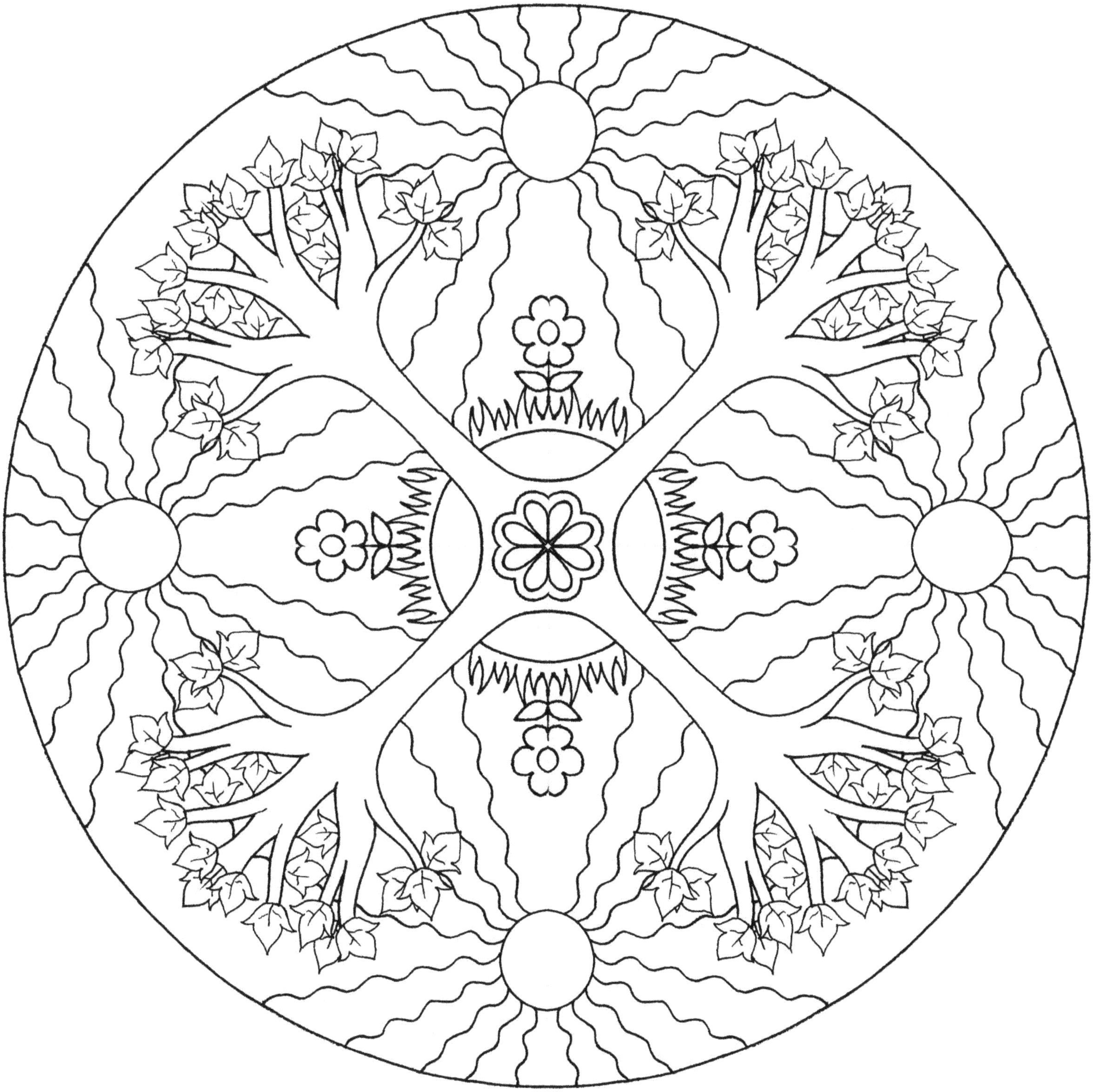

 facebook.com/tabbystangledart

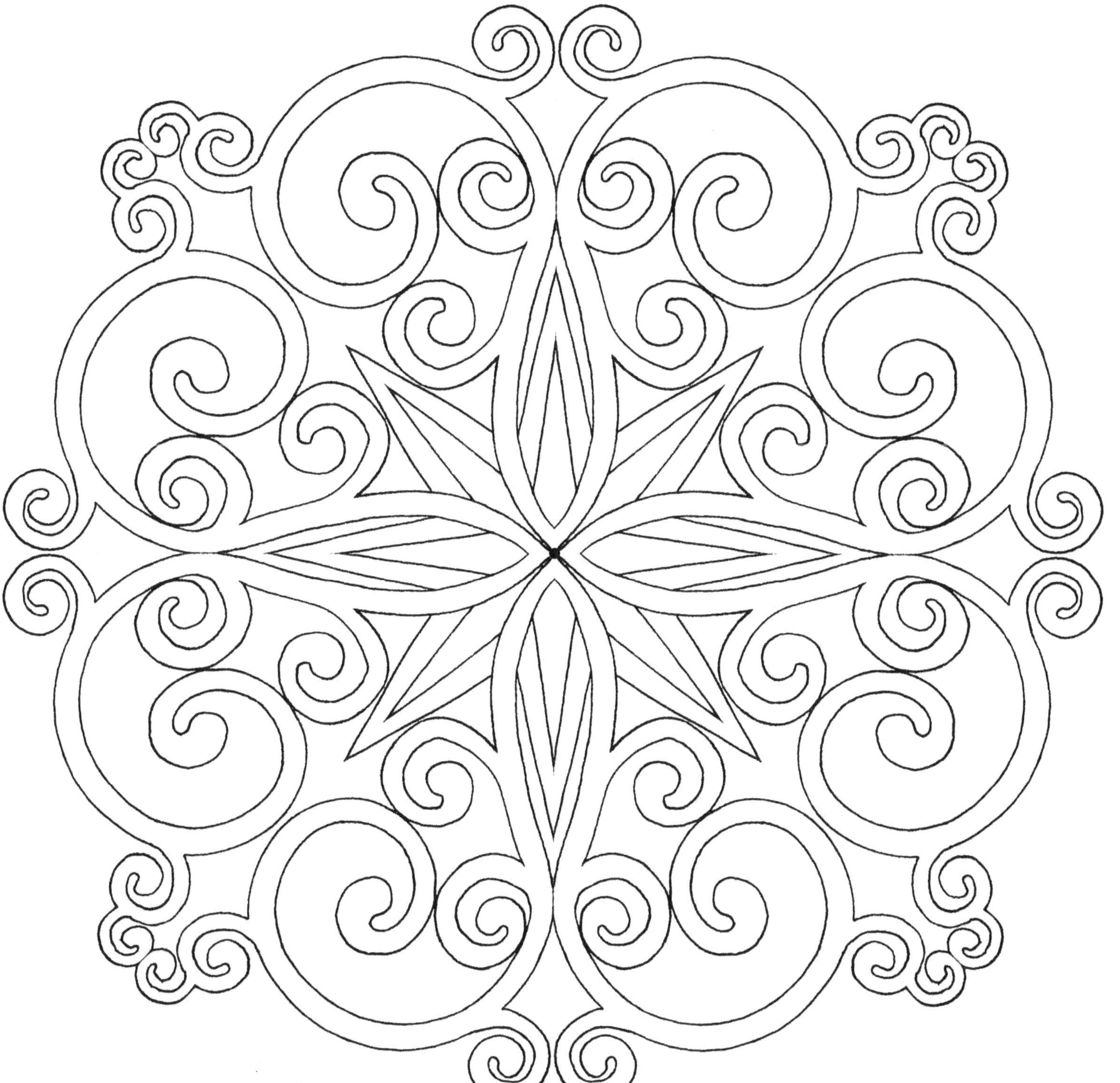

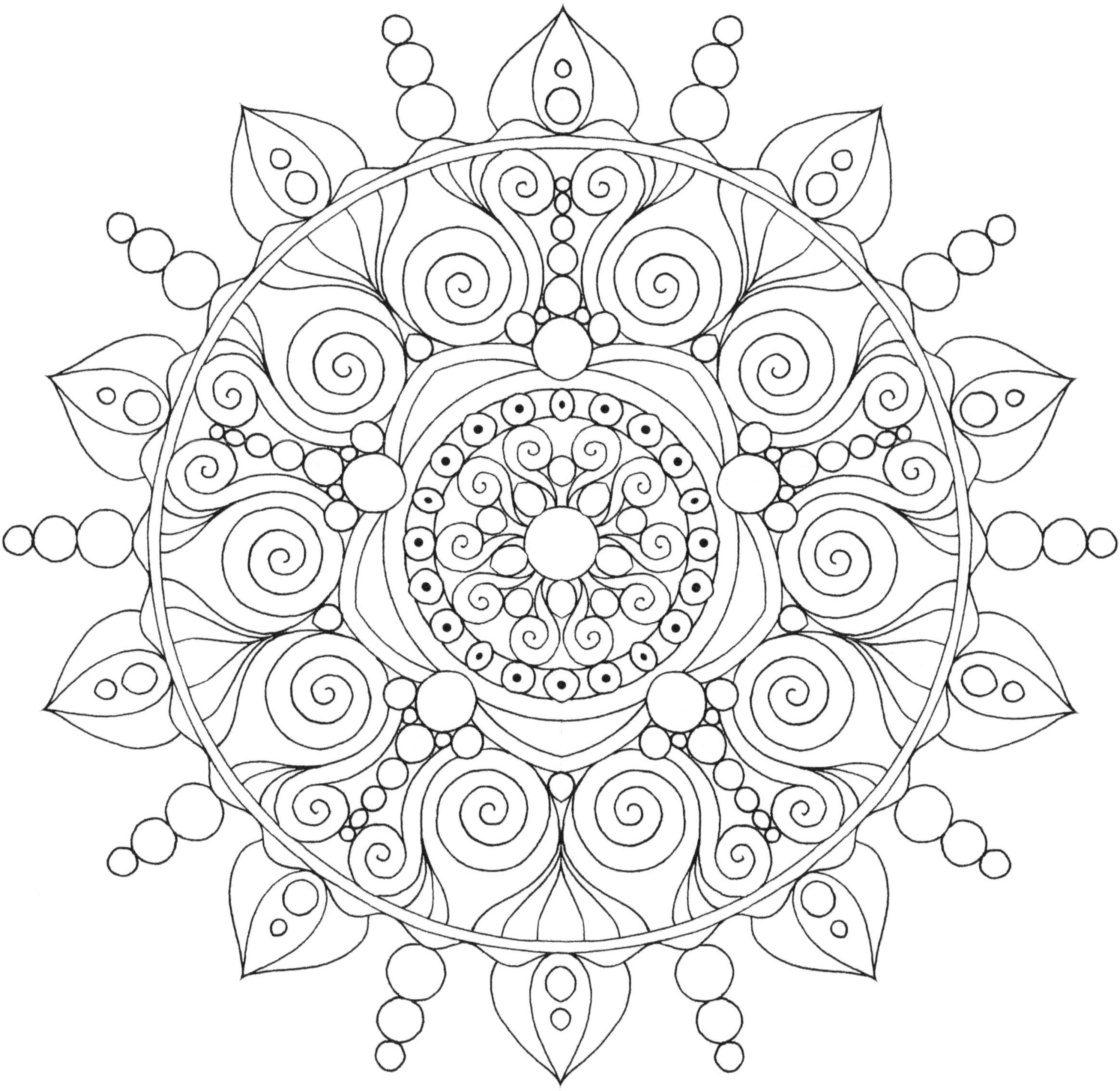

 facebook.com/tabbystangledart

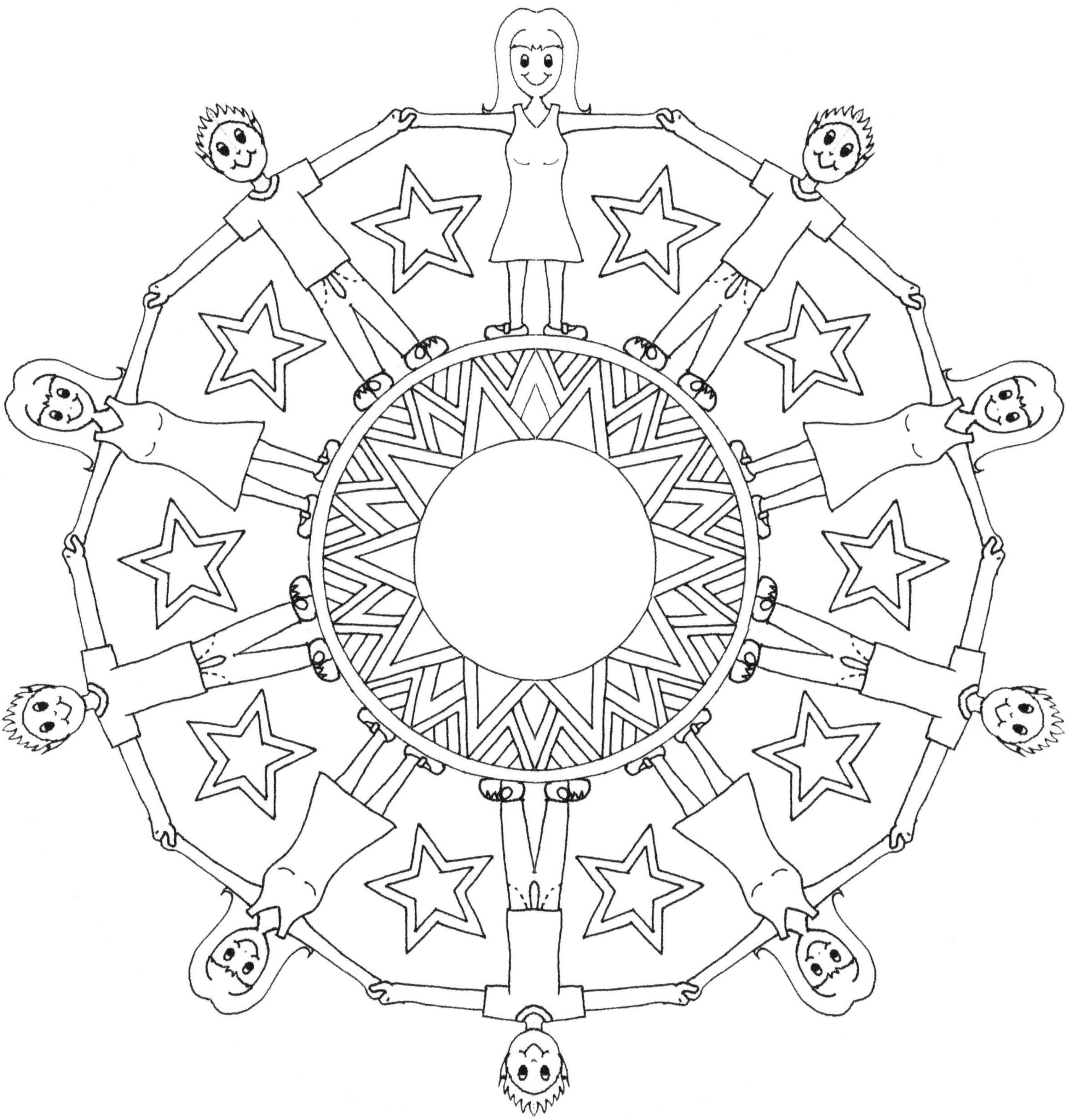

 facebook.com/tabbystangledart

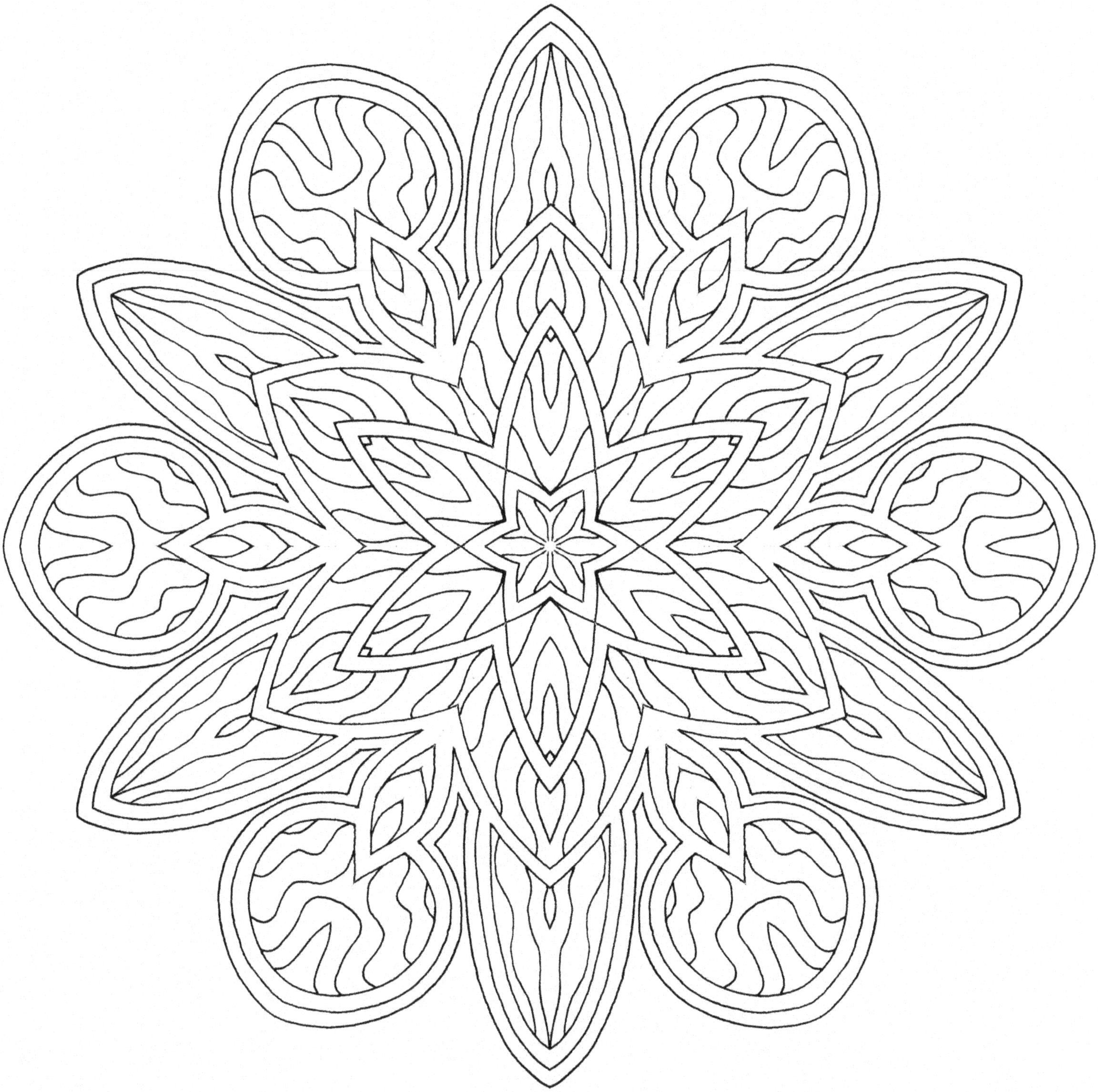

 facebook.com/tabbystangledart

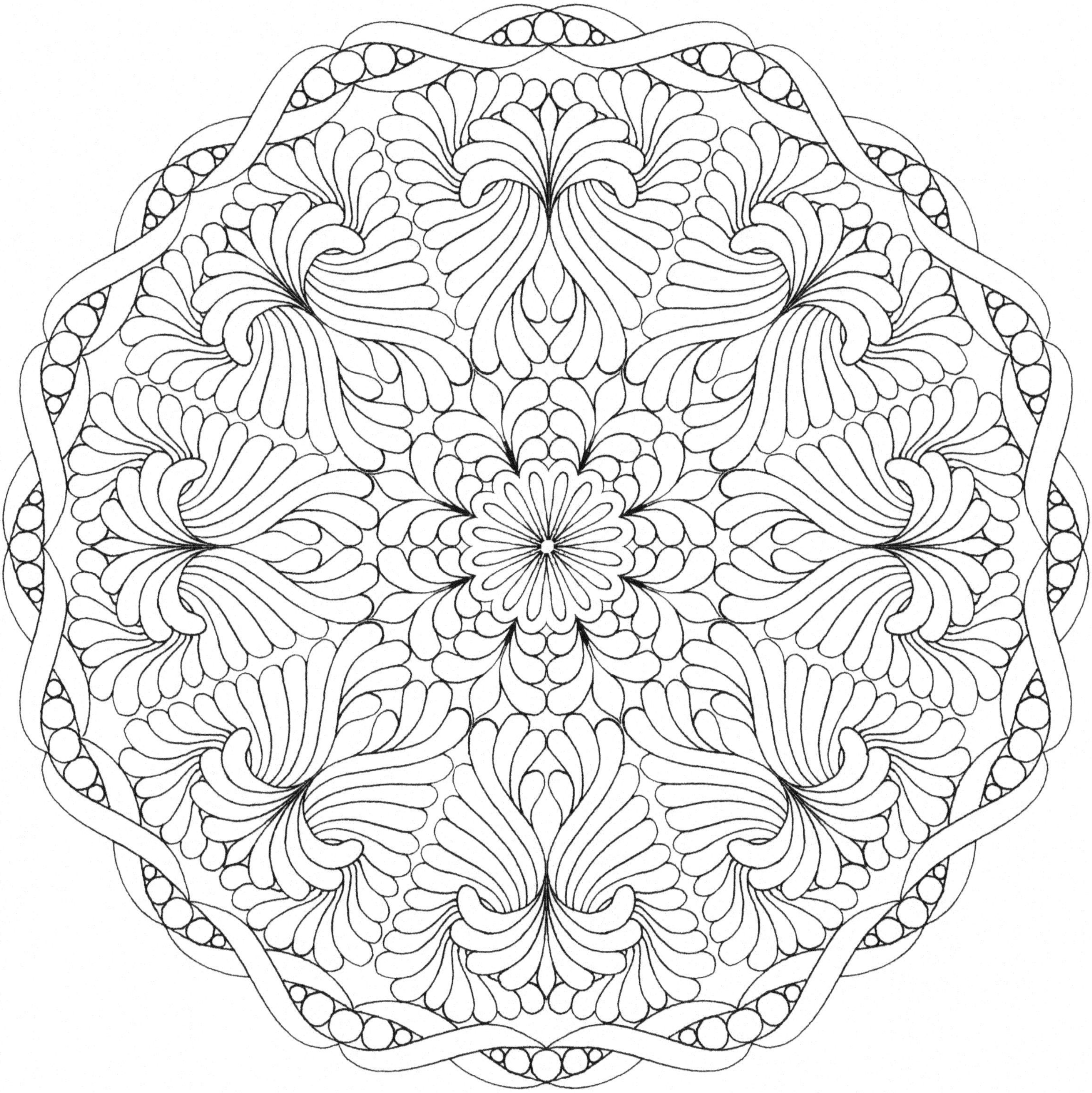

 facebook.com/tabbystangledart

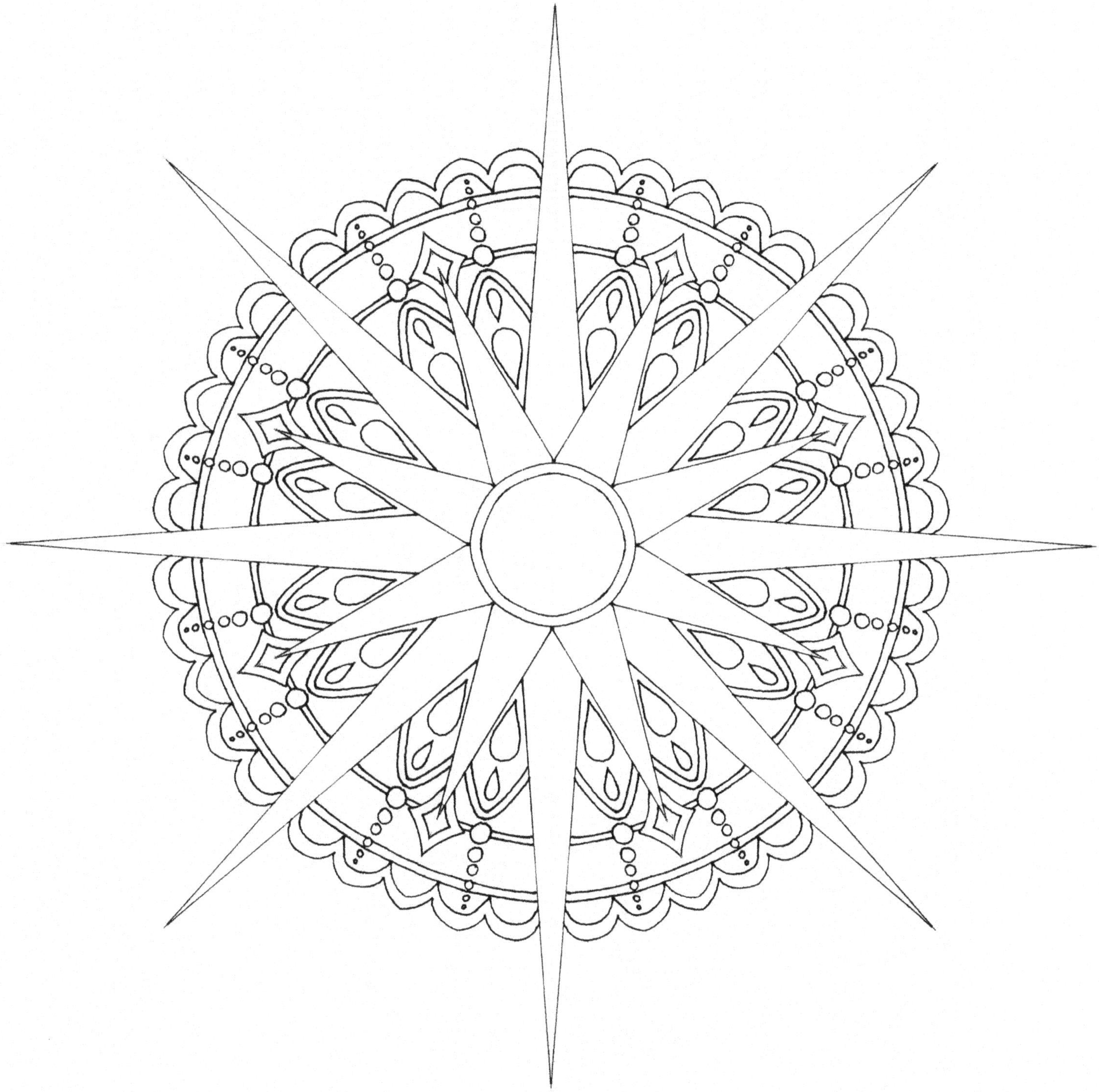

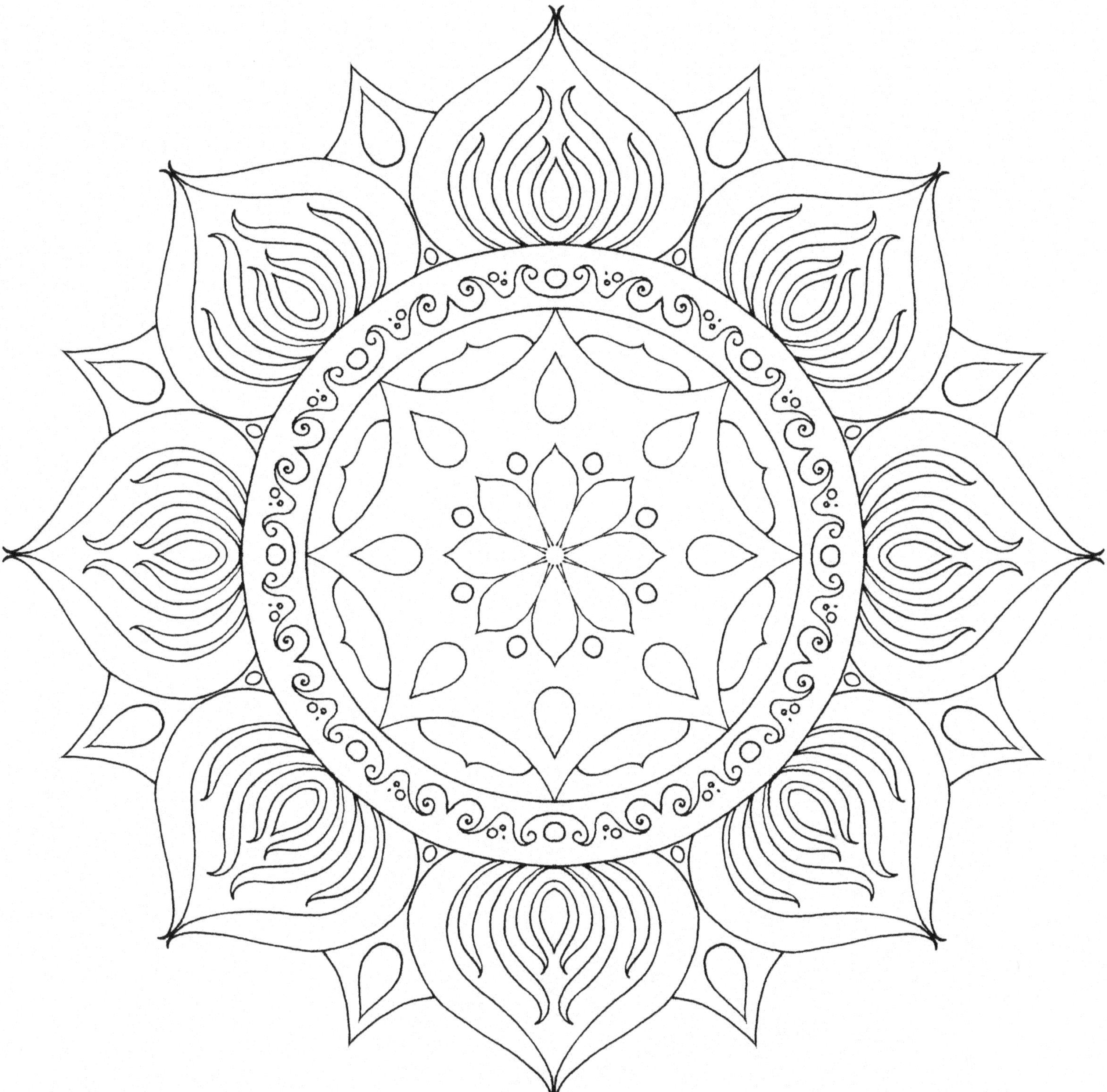

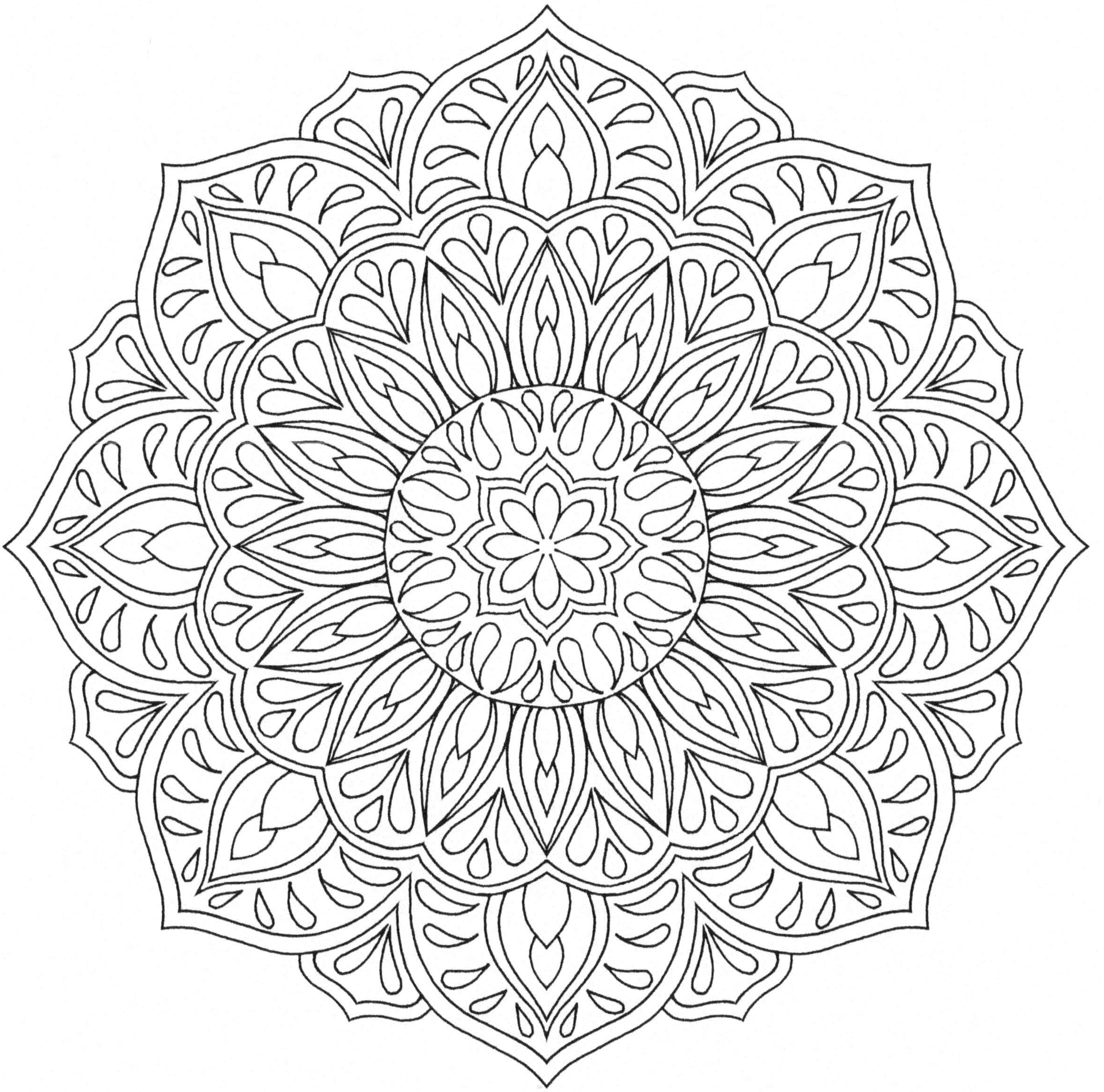

 facebook.com/tabbystangledart

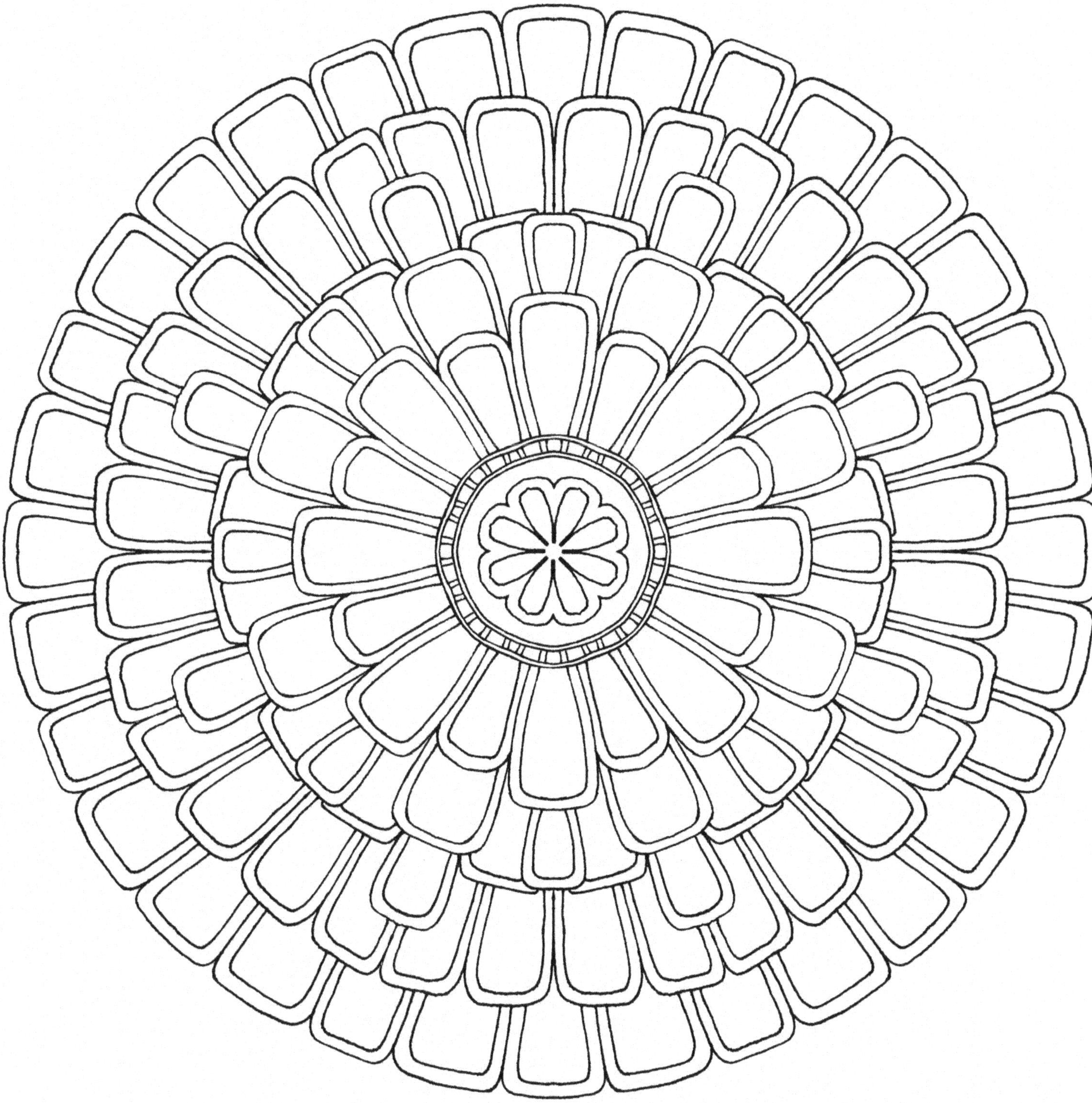

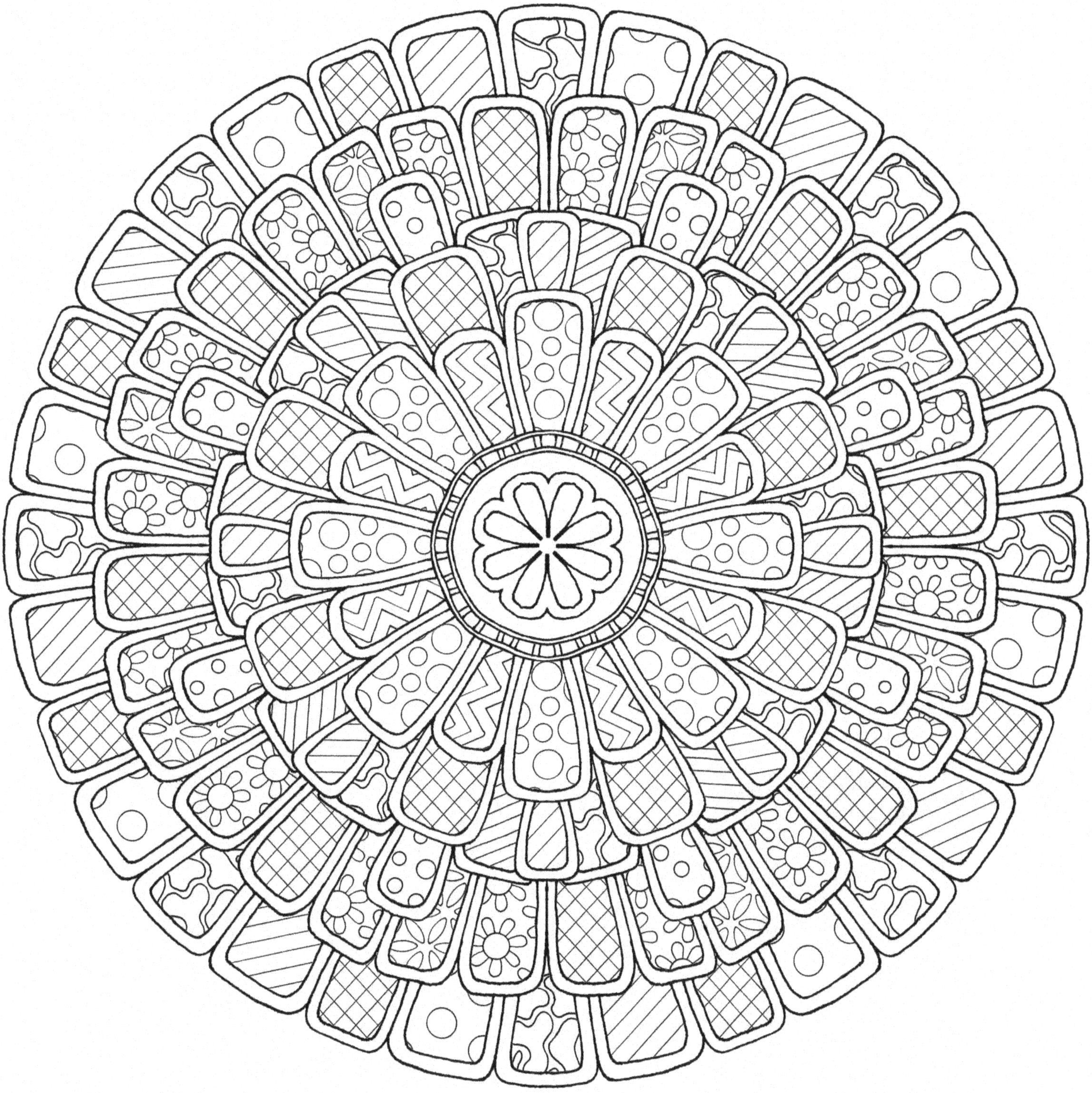

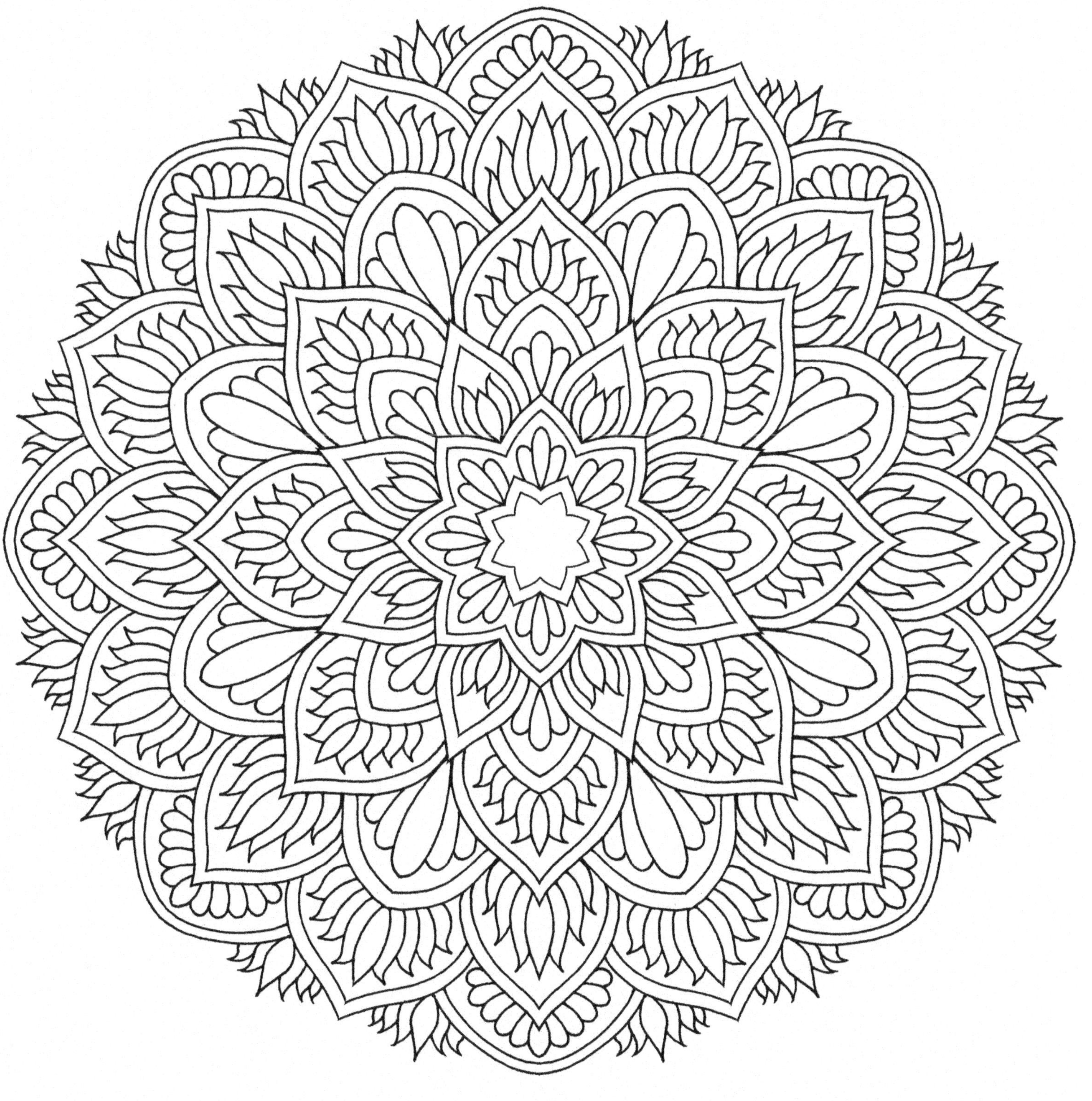

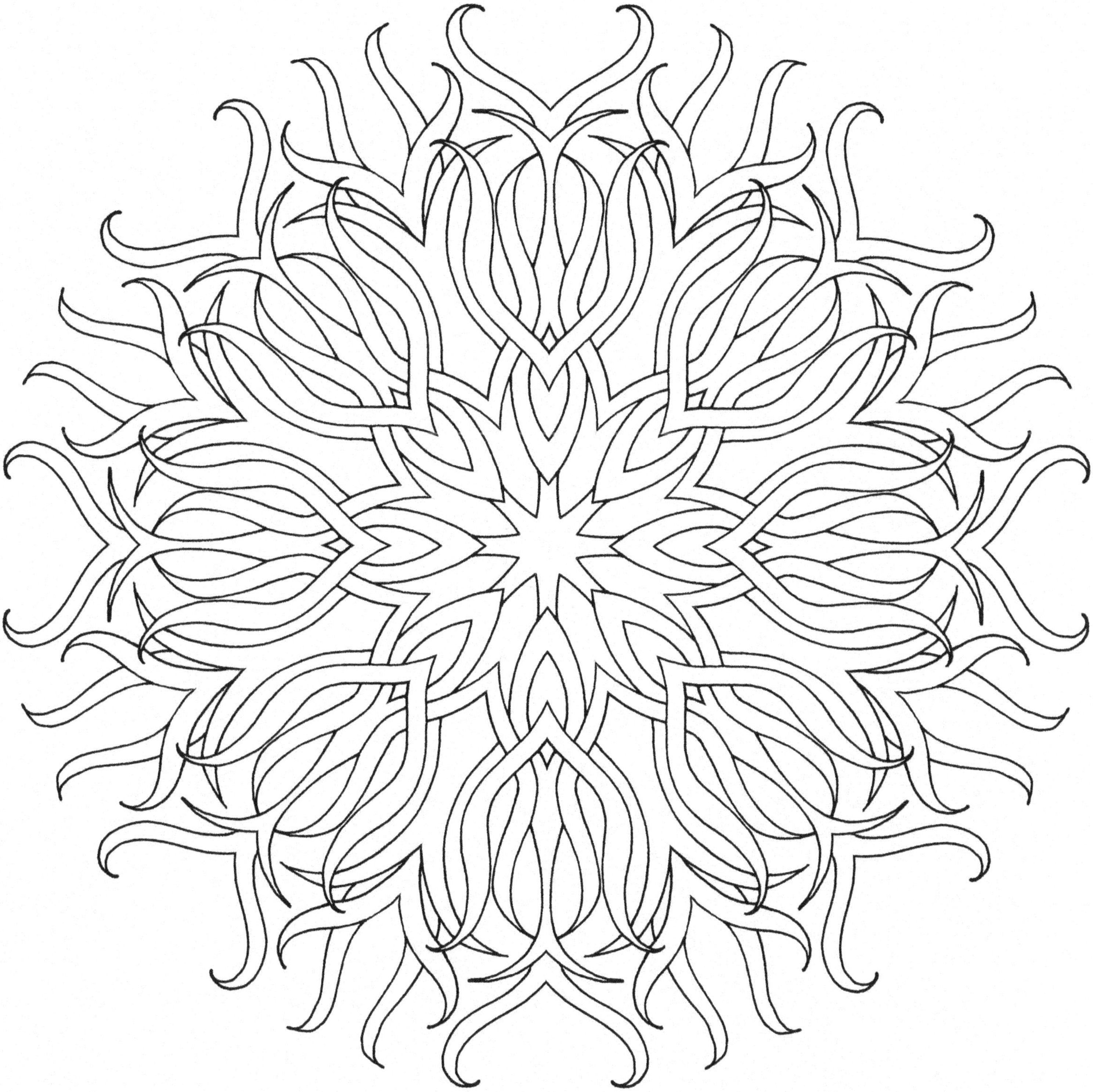

 facebook.com/tabbystangledart

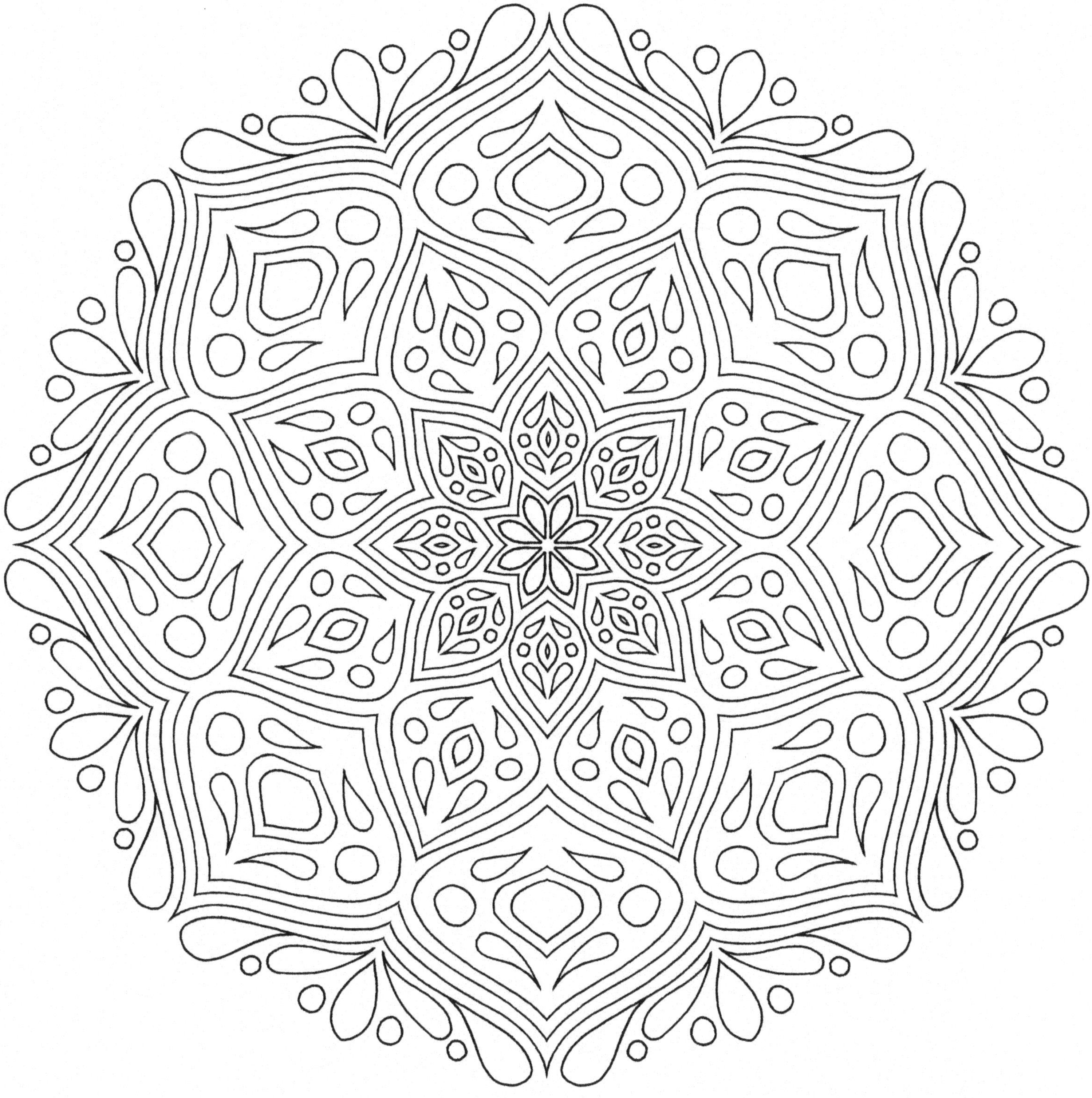

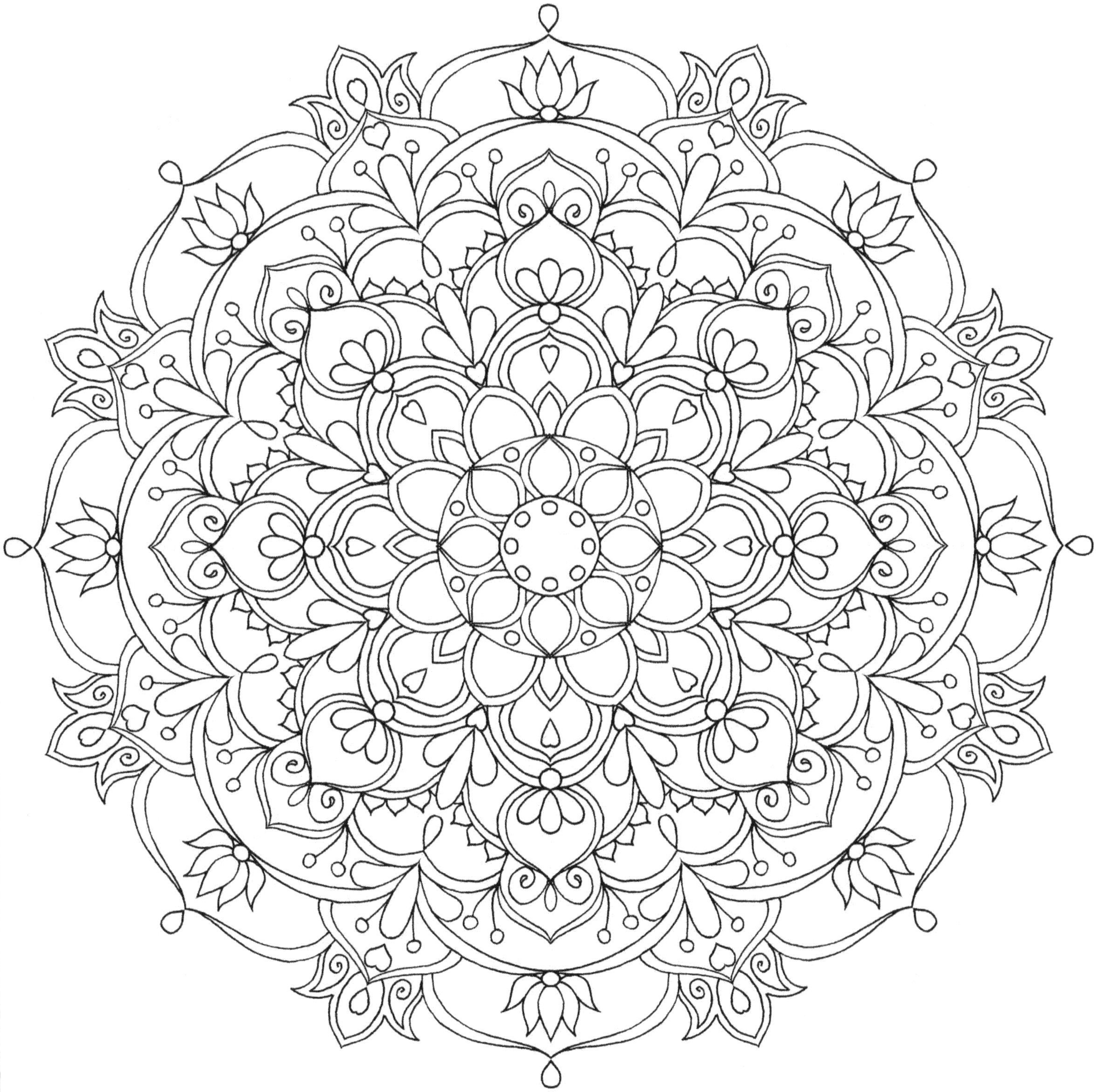

 facebook.com/tabbystangledart

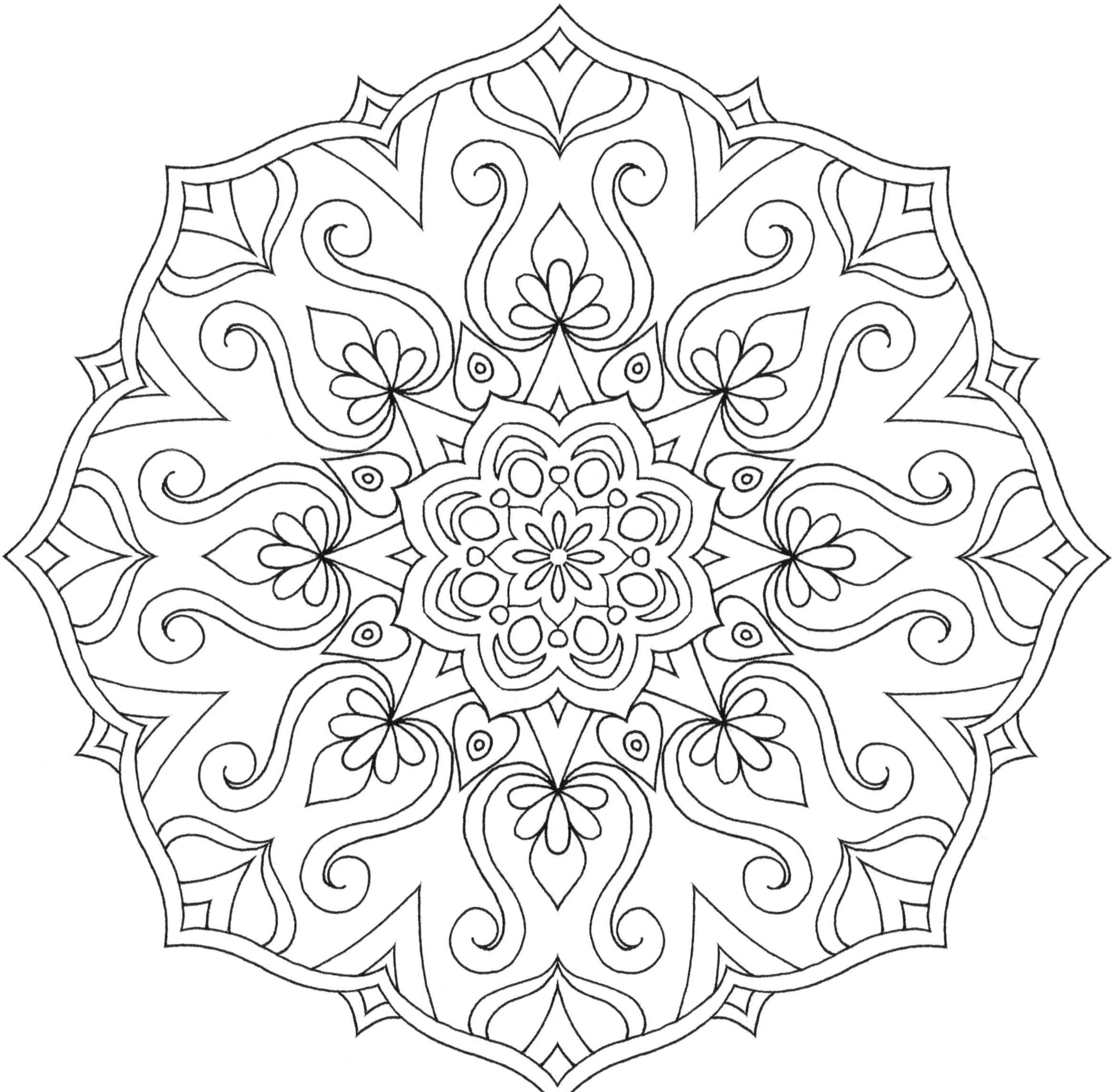

 facebook.com/tabbystangledart

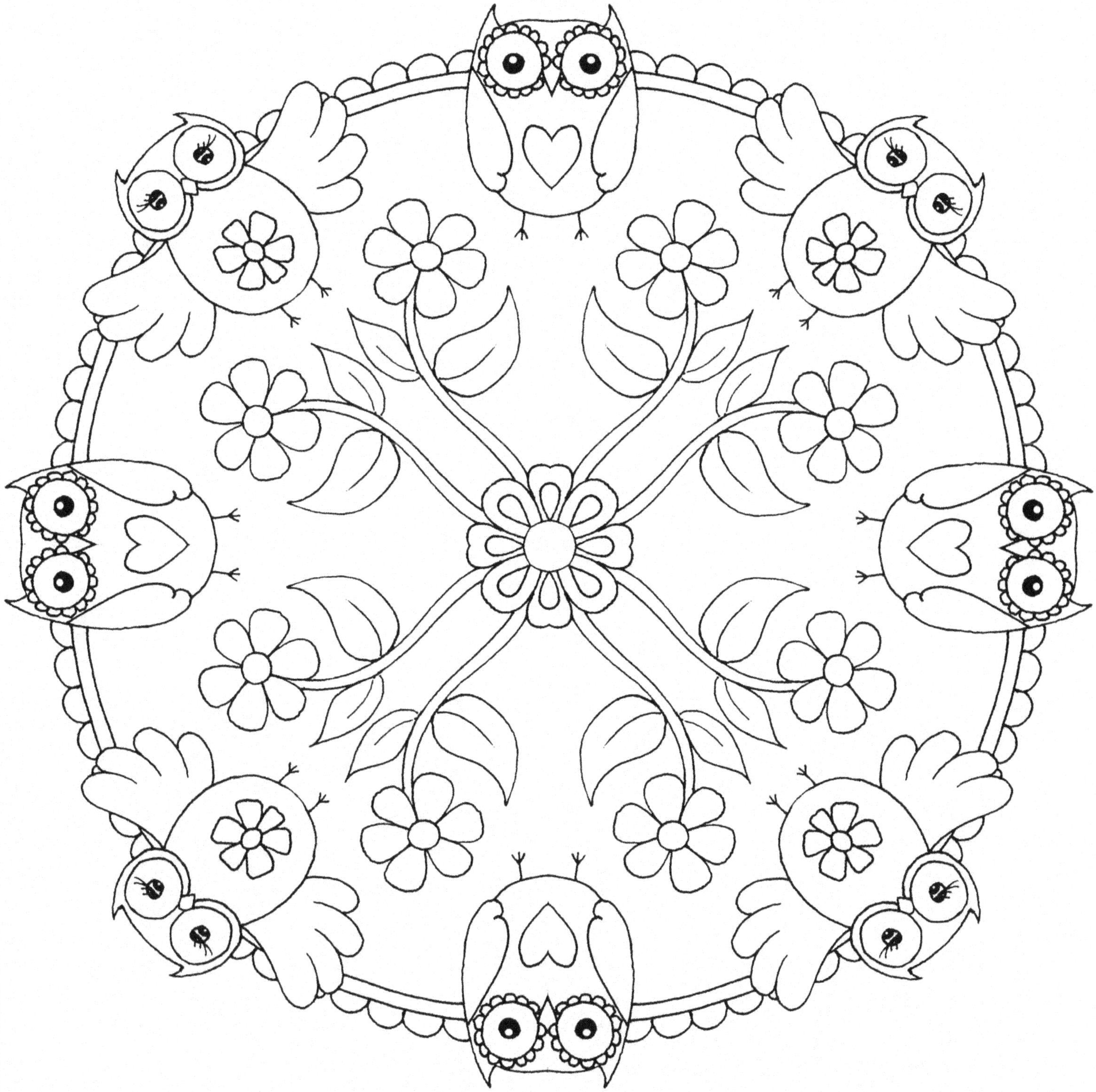

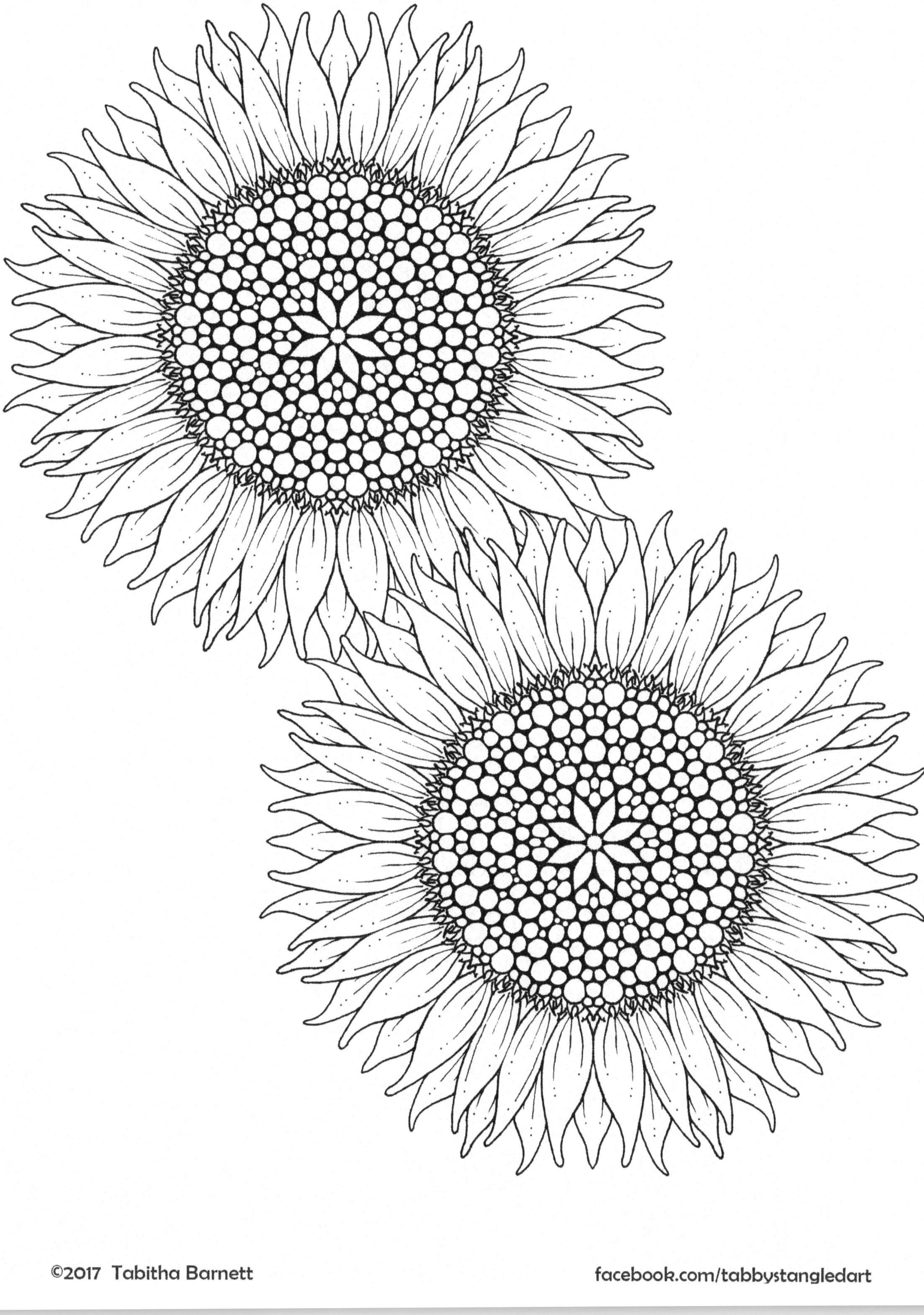

Color Test Sheet

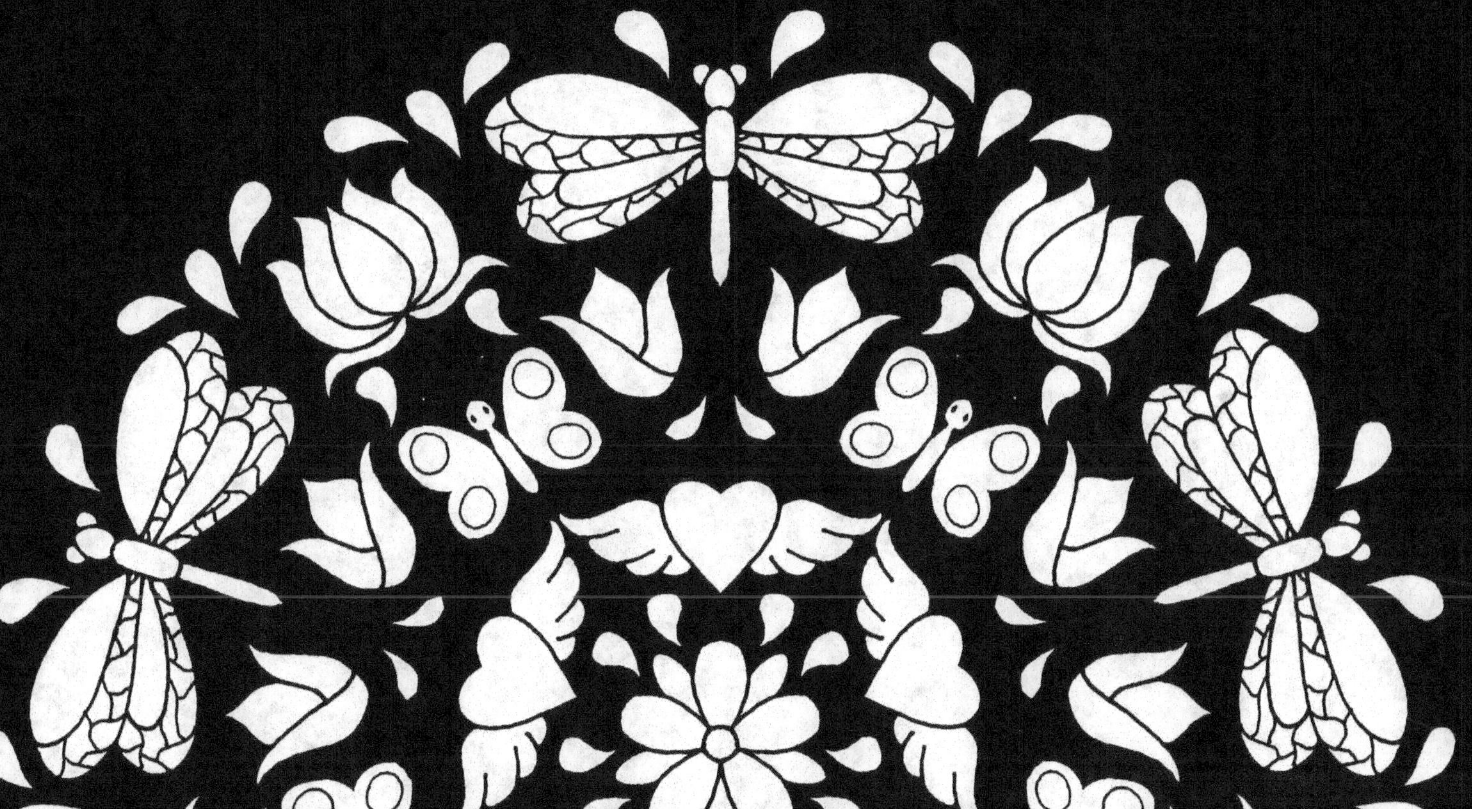

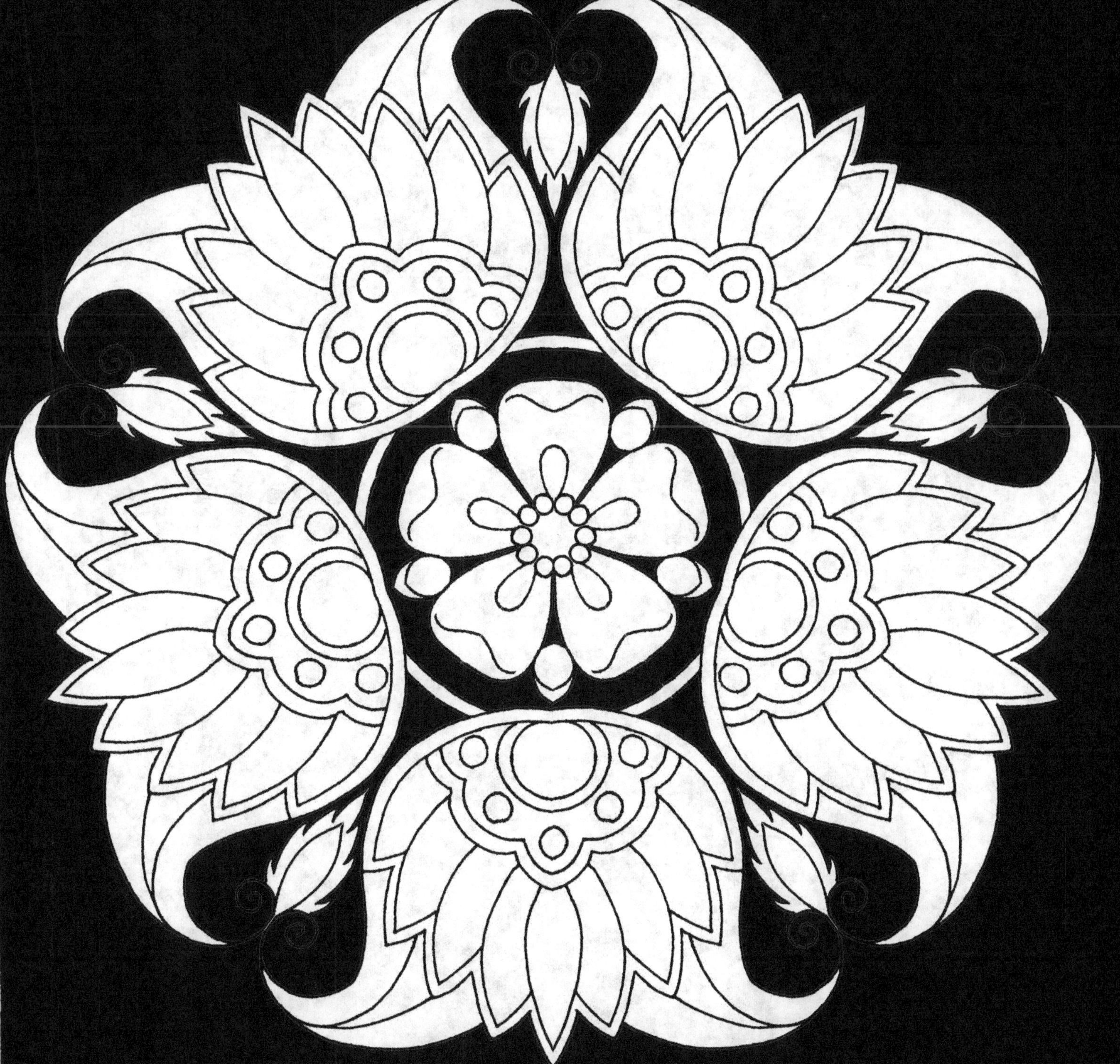

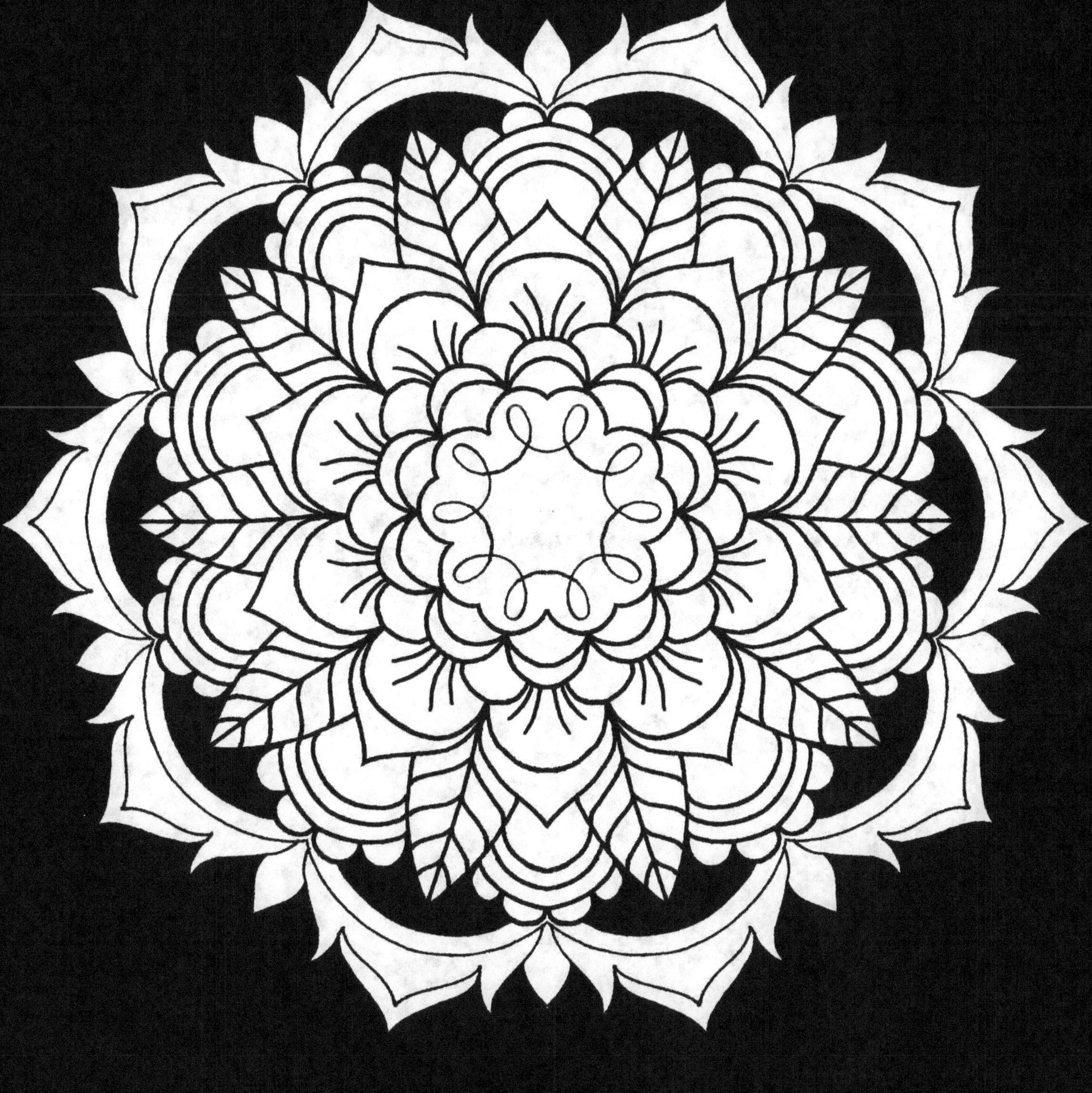

 facebook.com/tabbystangledart

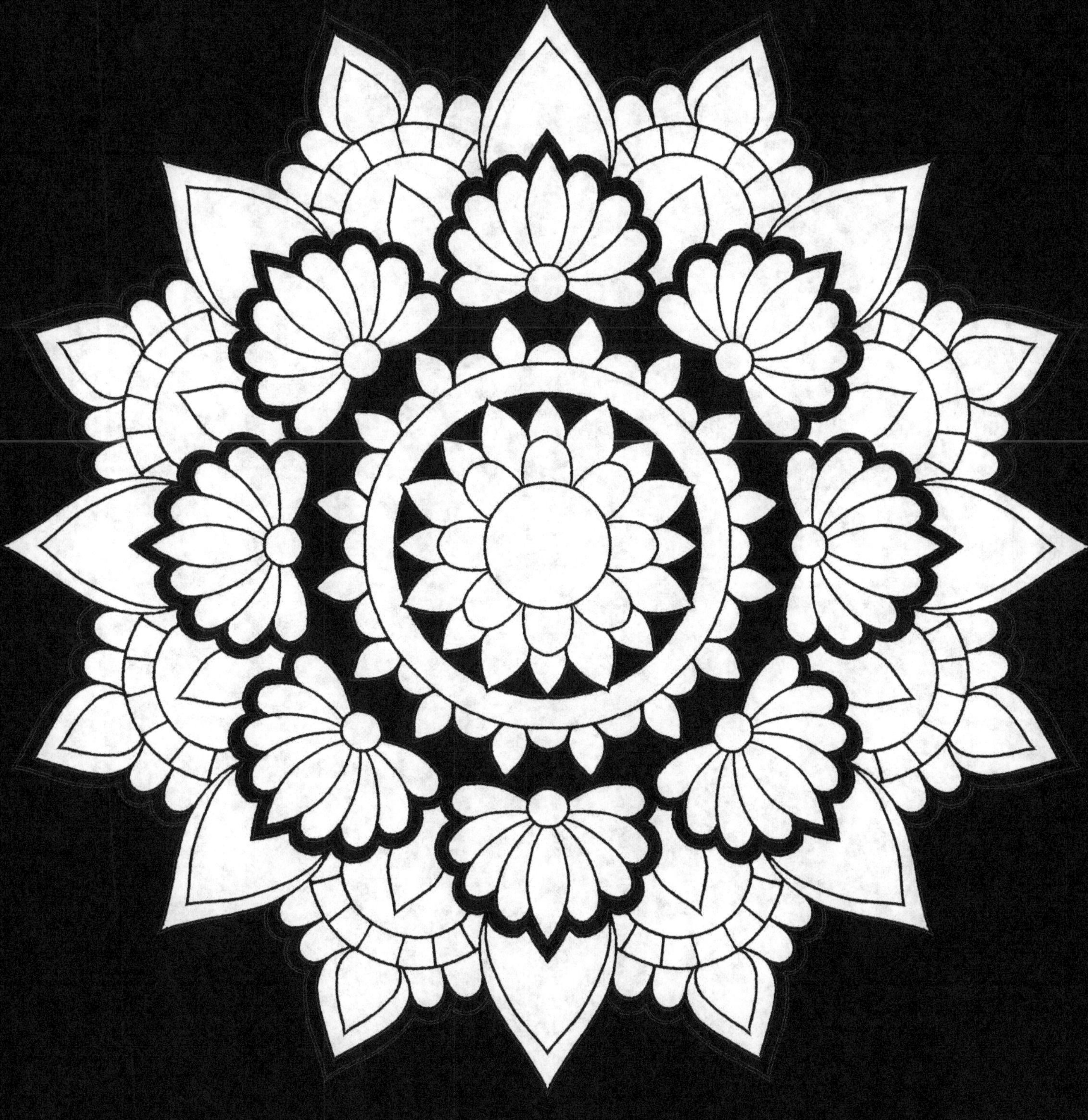

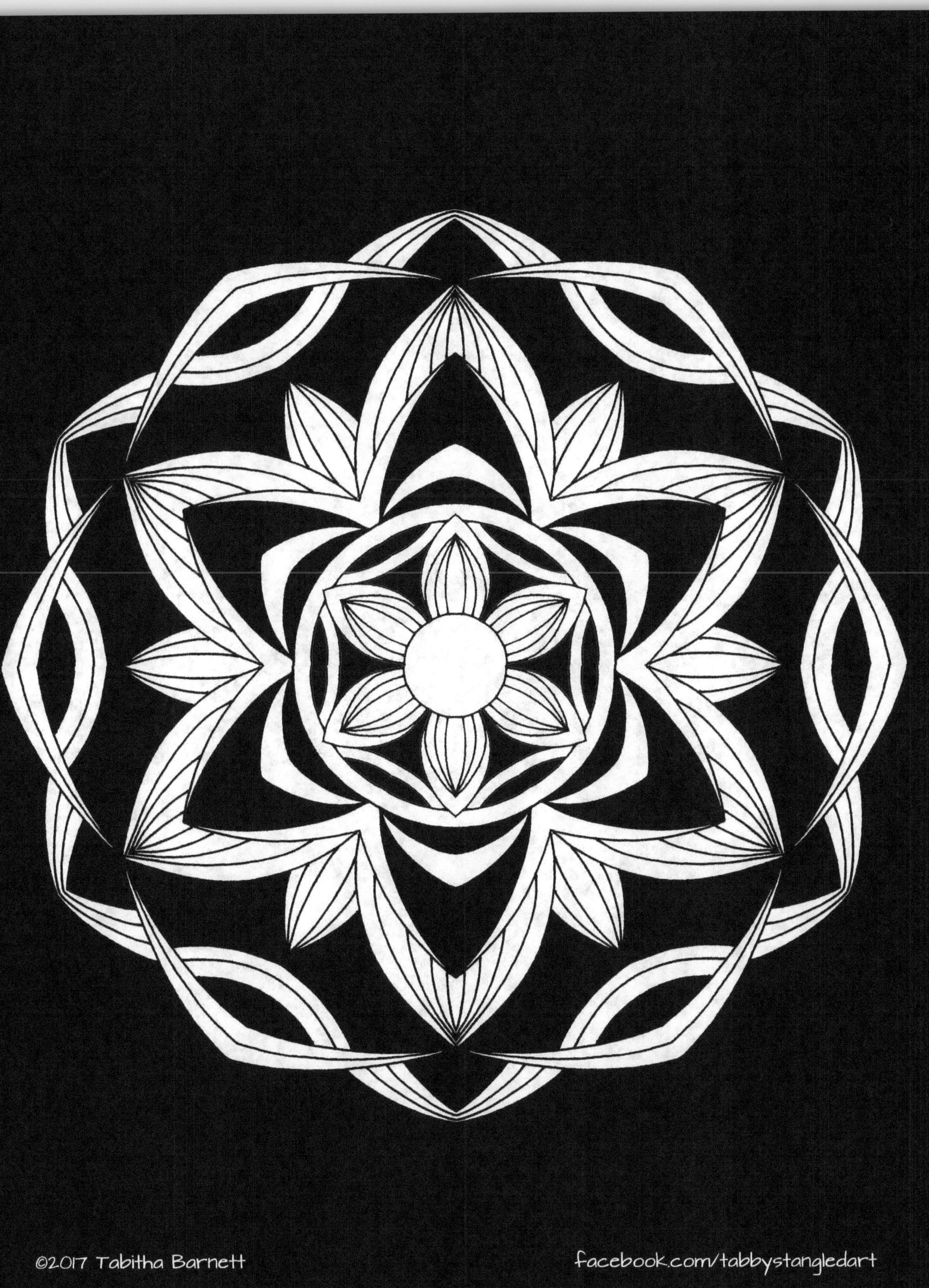

 facebook.com/tabbystangledart

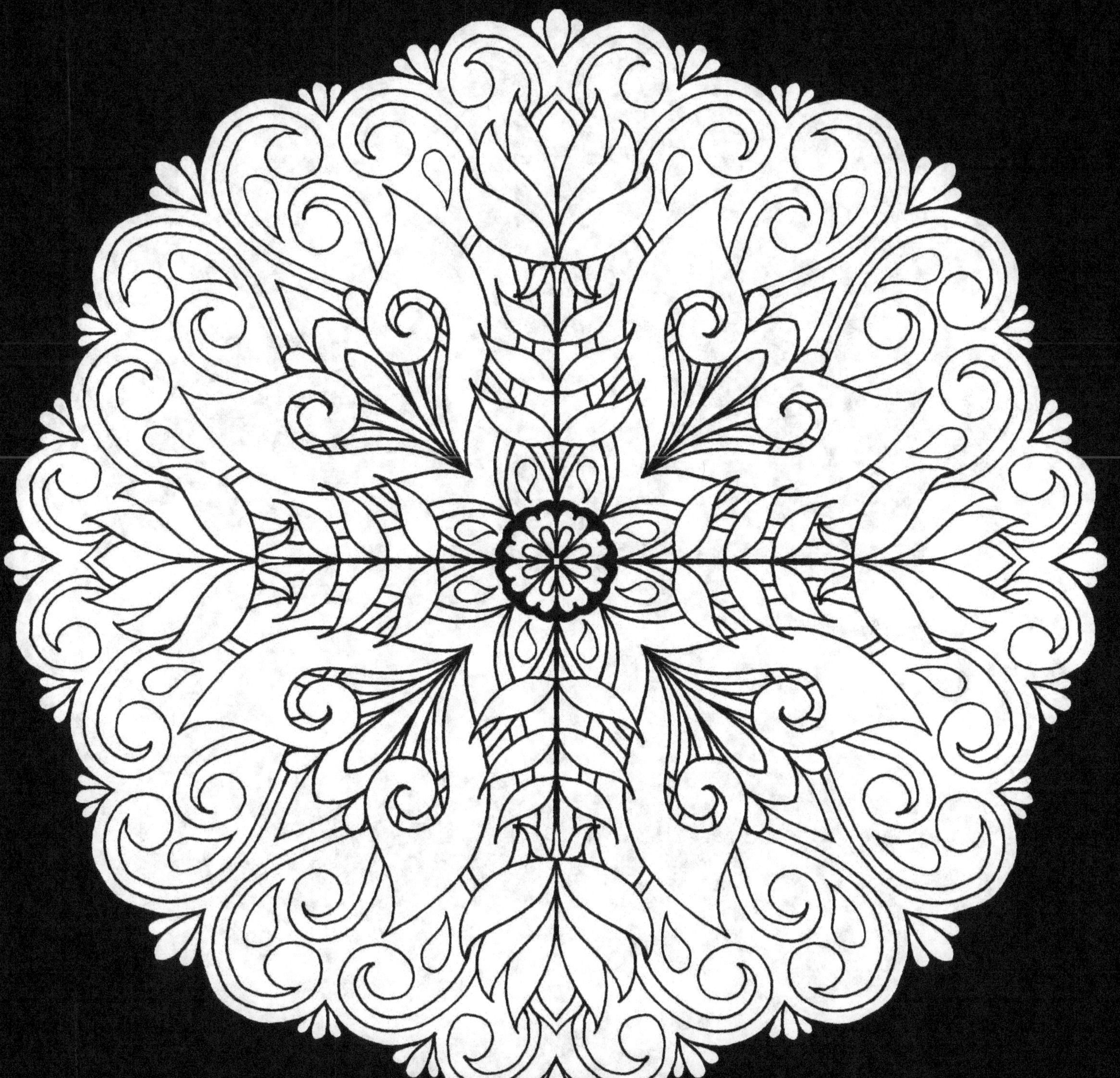

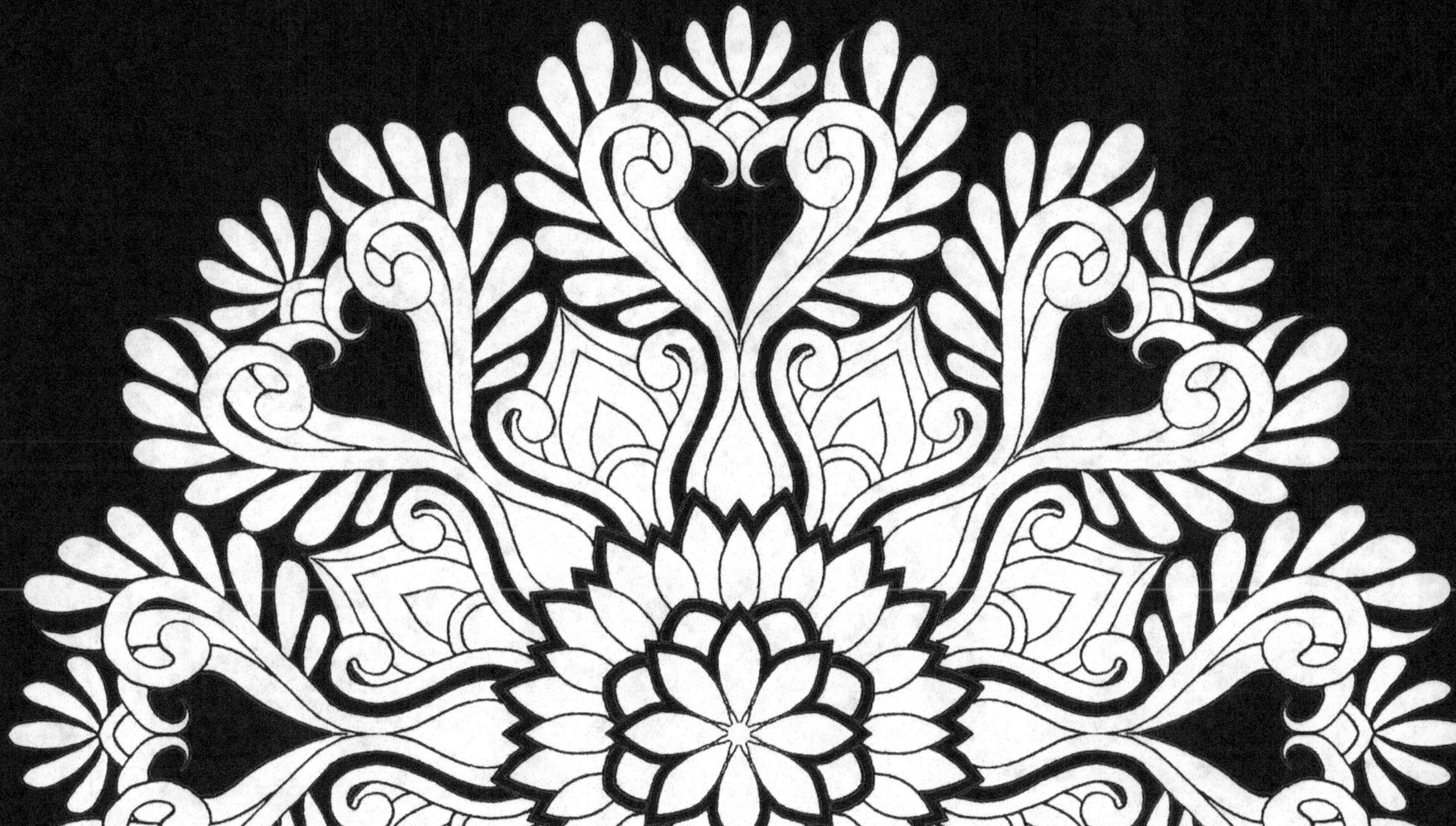

 facebook.com/tabbystangledart

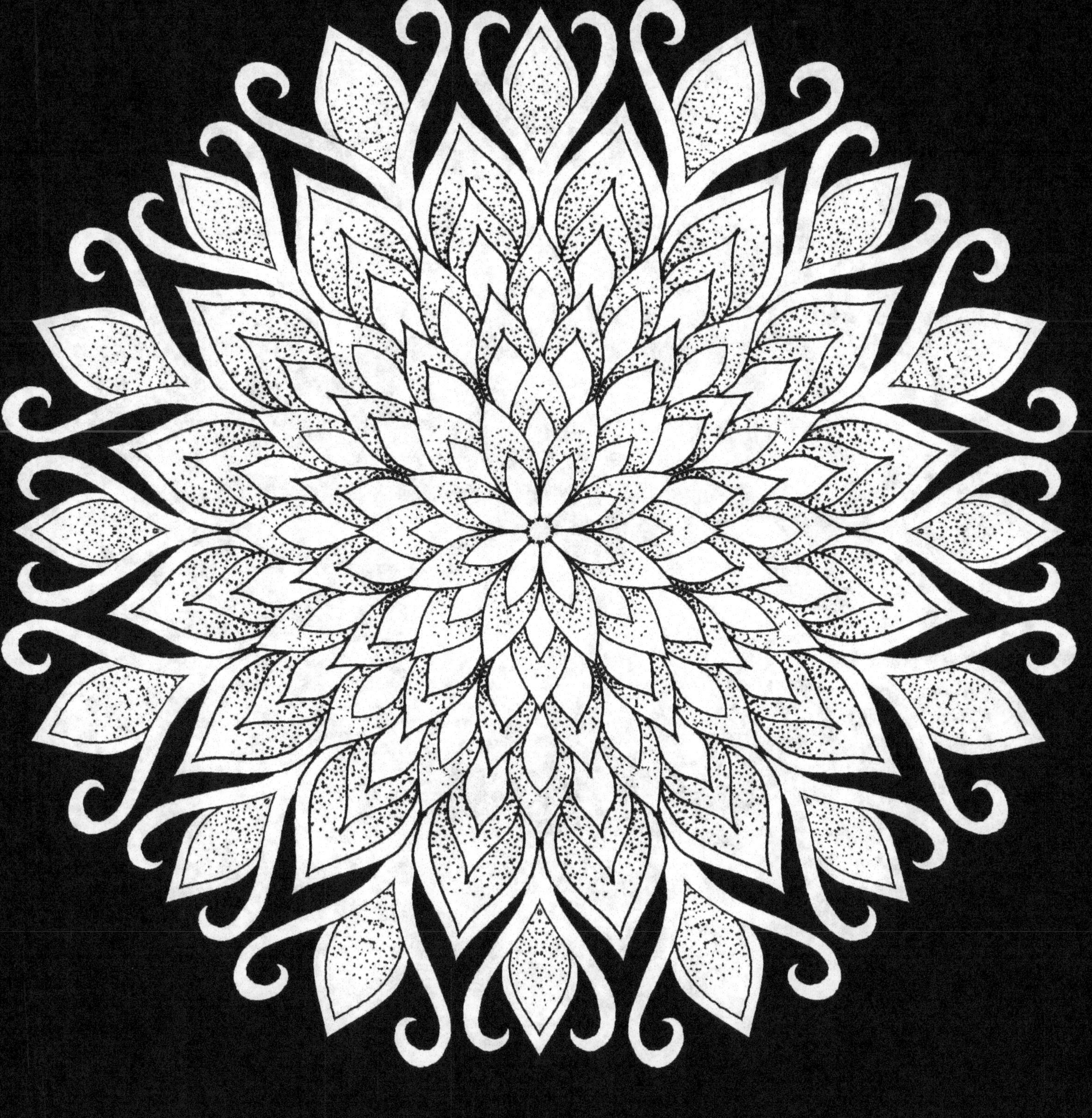

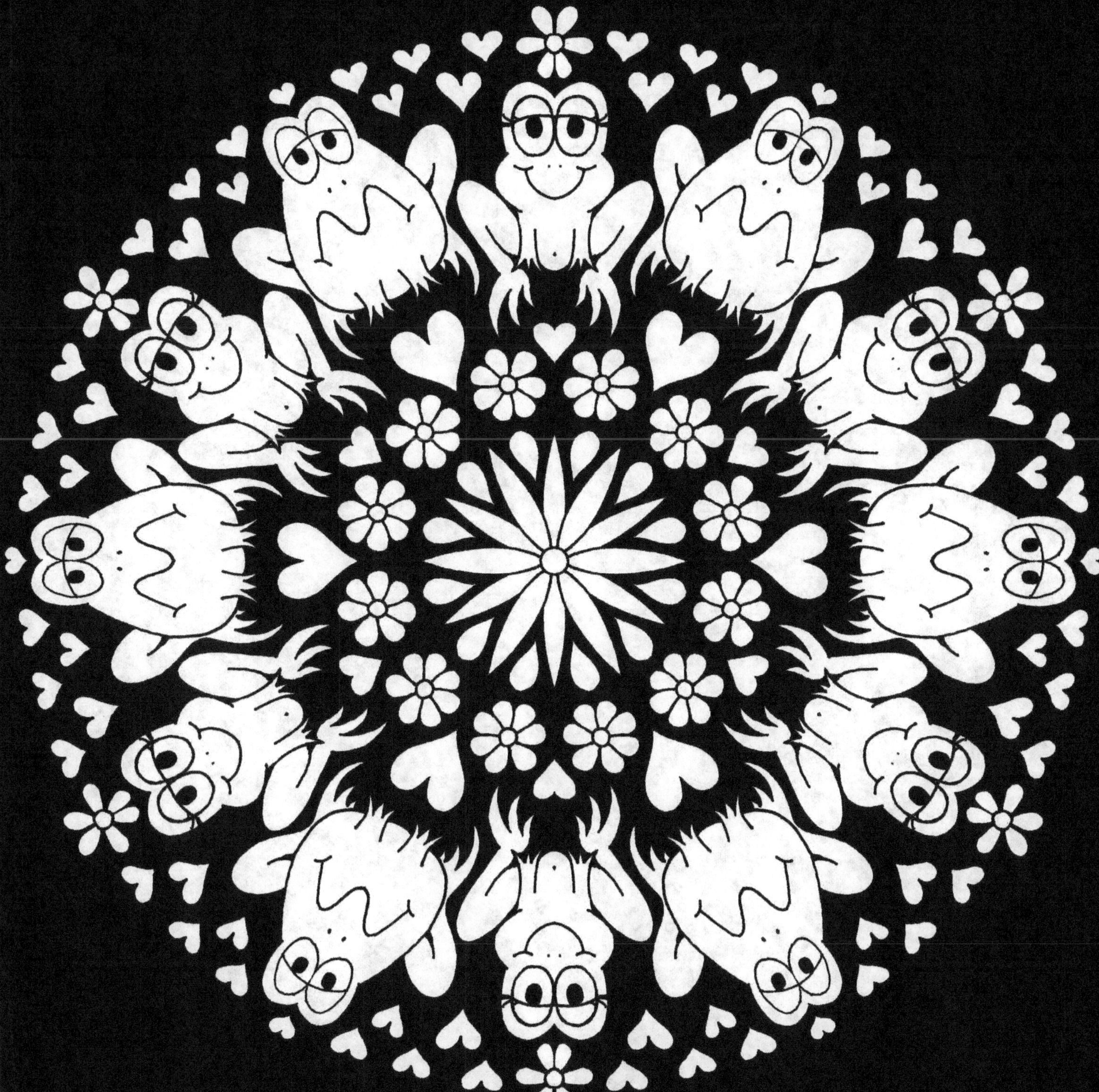

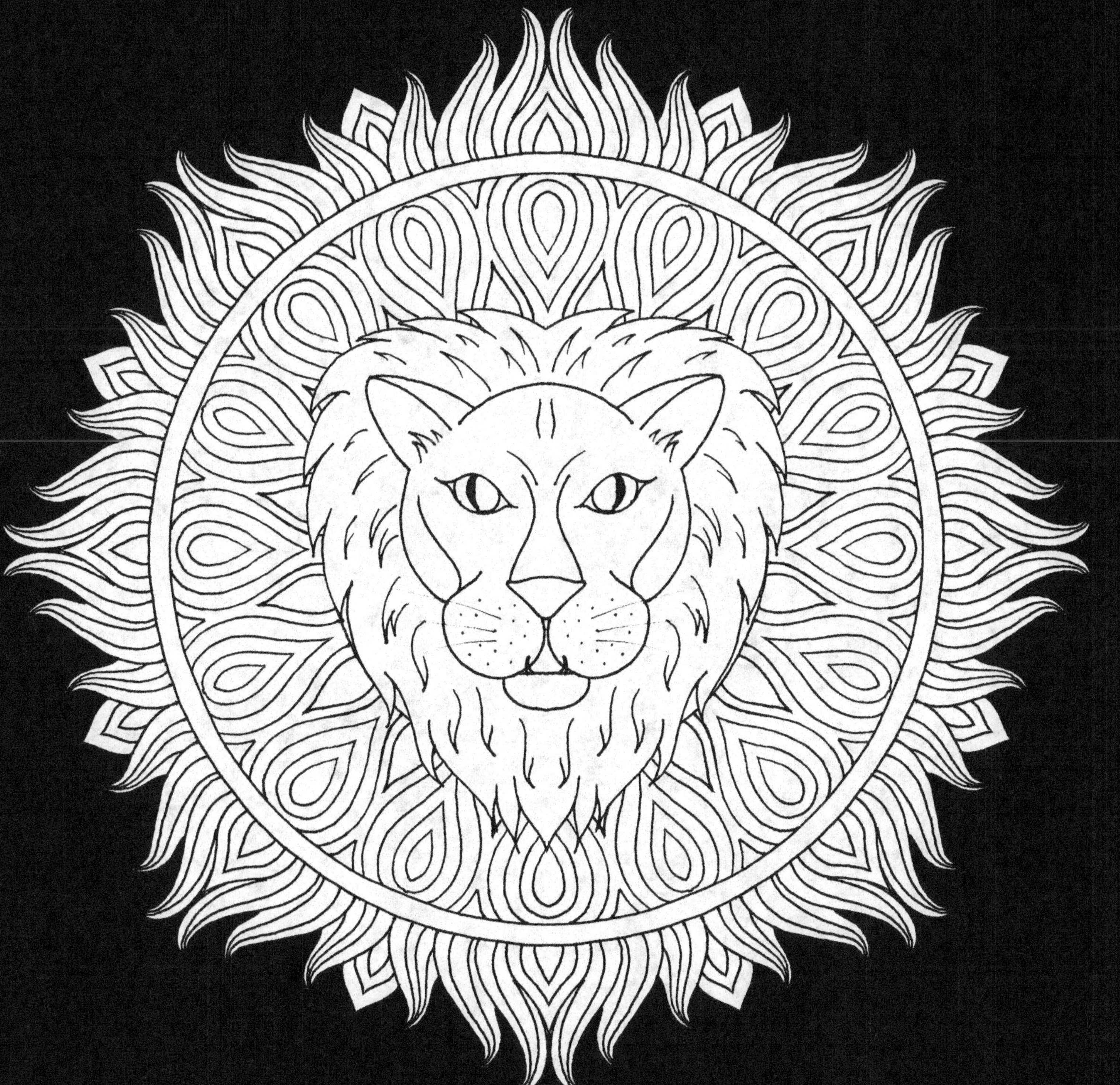

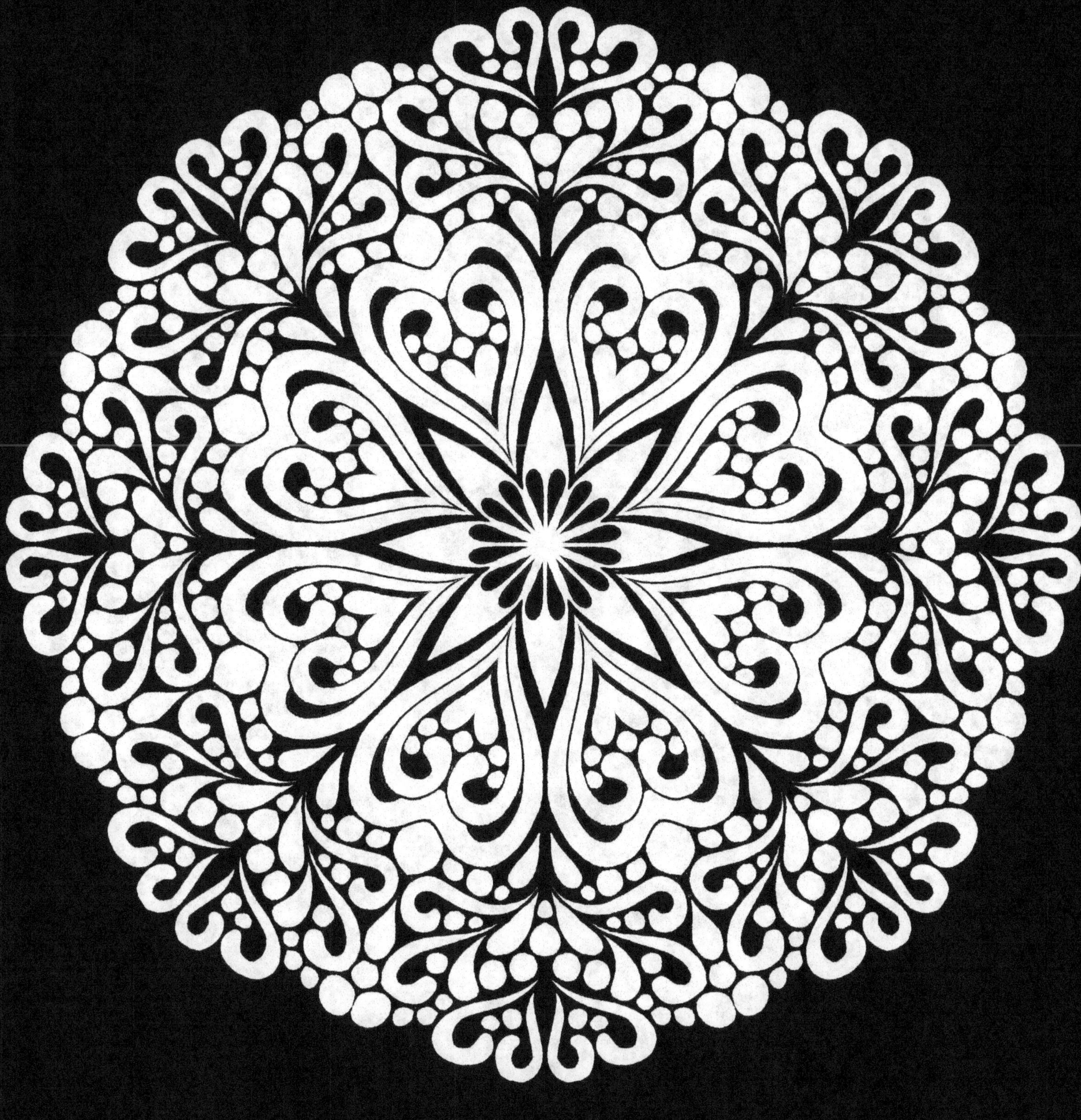

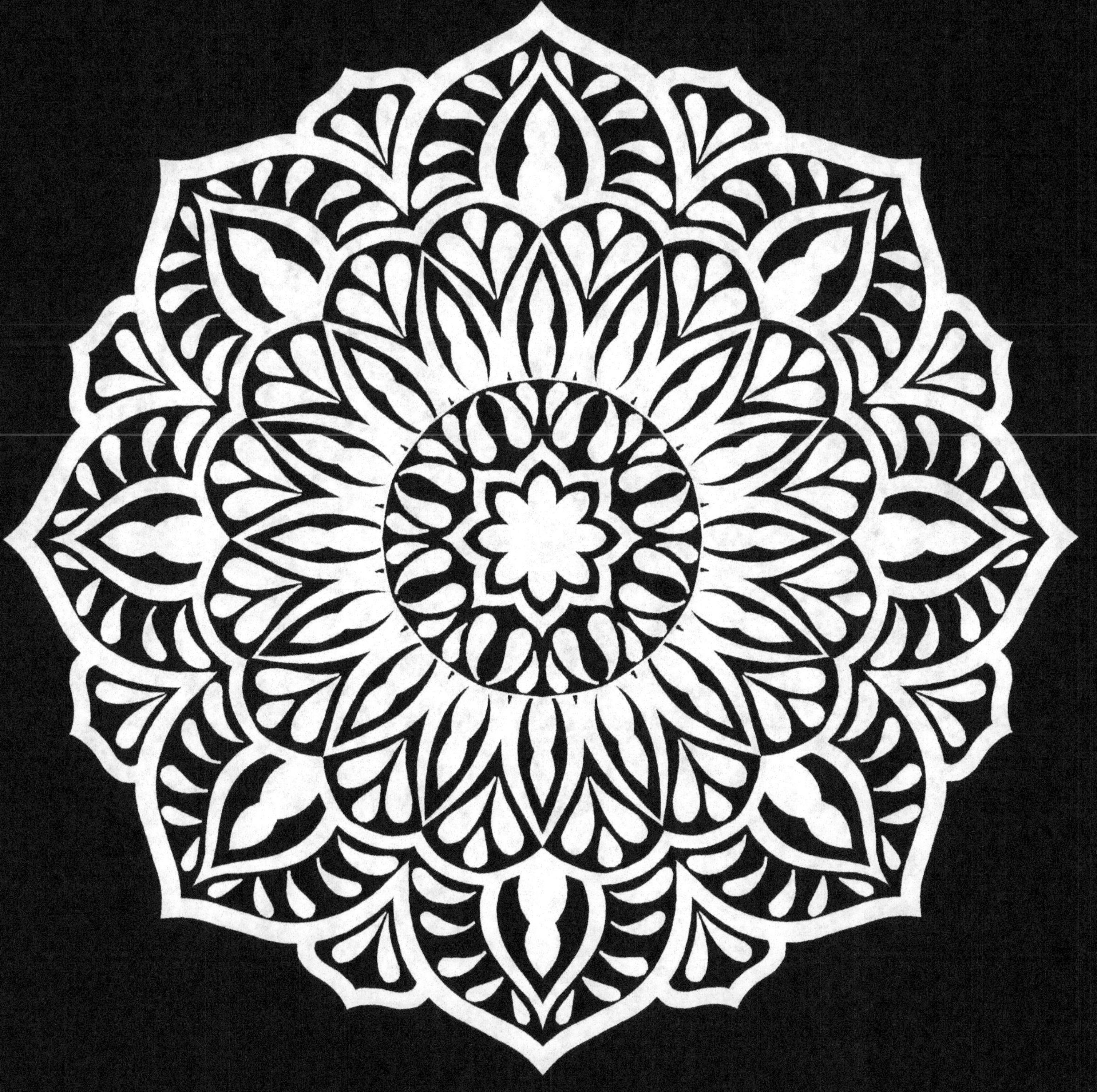

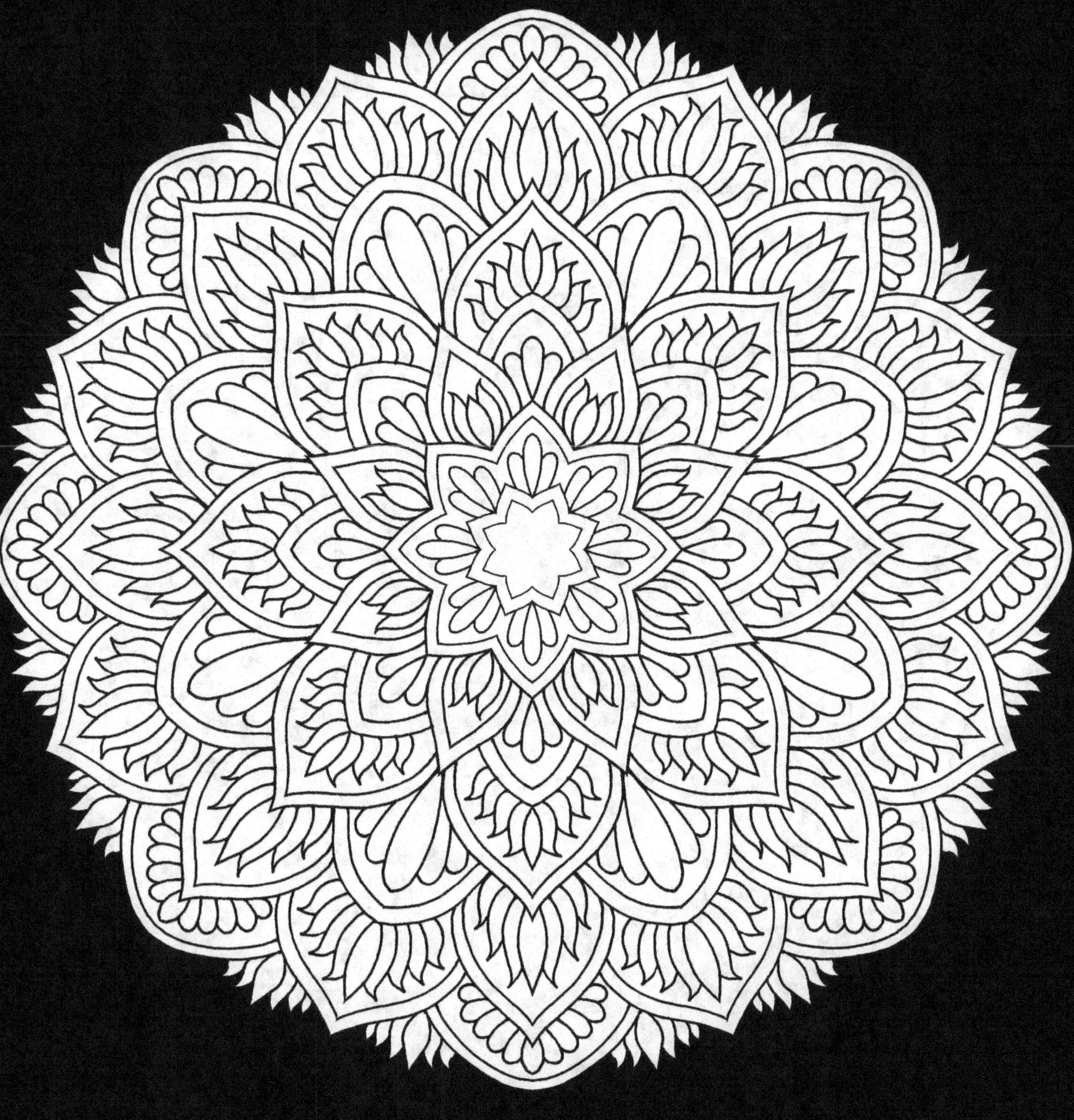

 facebook.com/tabbystangledart

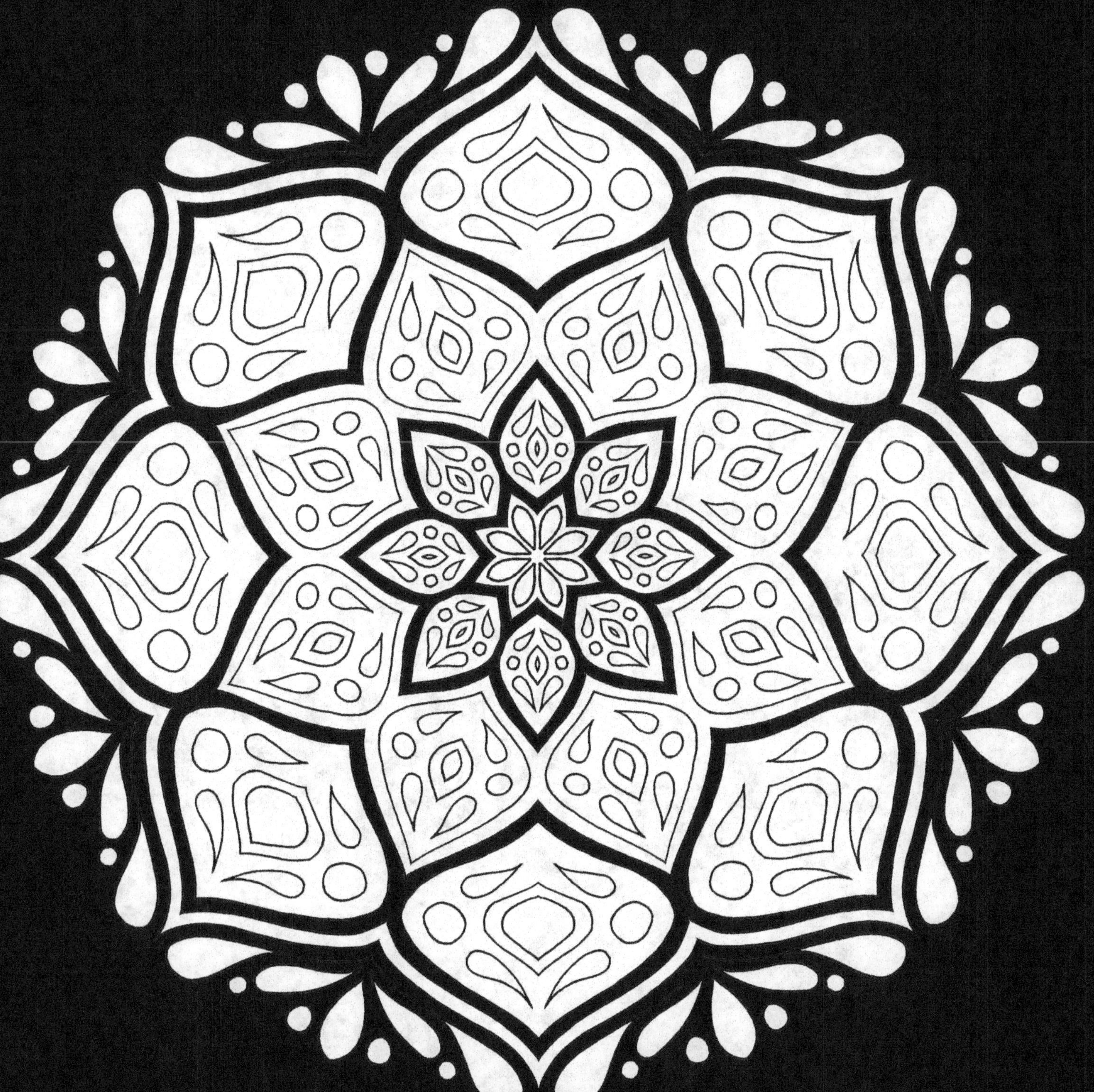

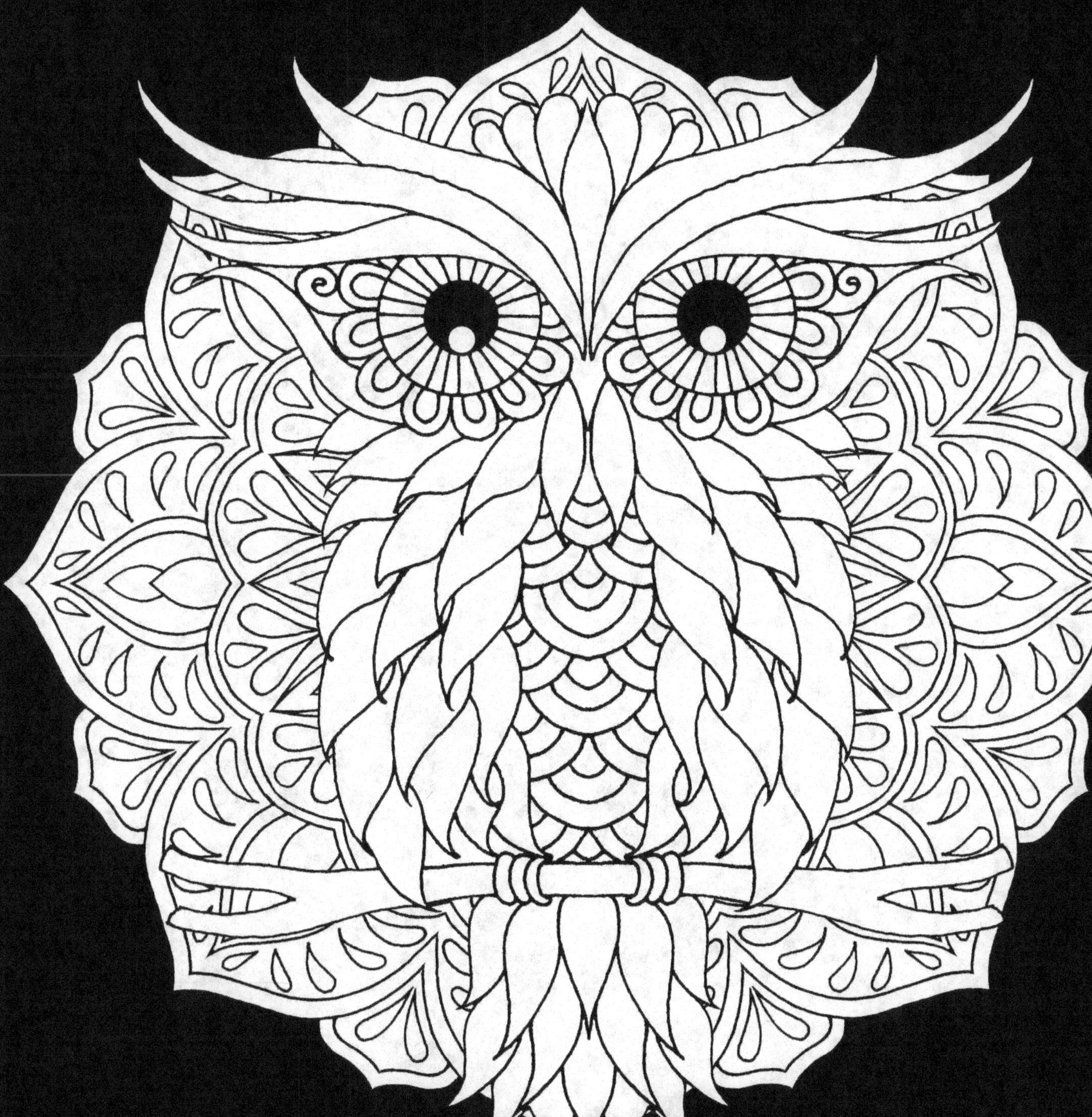

facebook.com/tabbystangledart

 facebook.com/tabbystangledart

Color Test Sheet

Join the conversation on facebook:

www.facebook.com/tabbystangledart

If you enjoyed this book, please consider taking a few minutes to leave a review on Amazon.

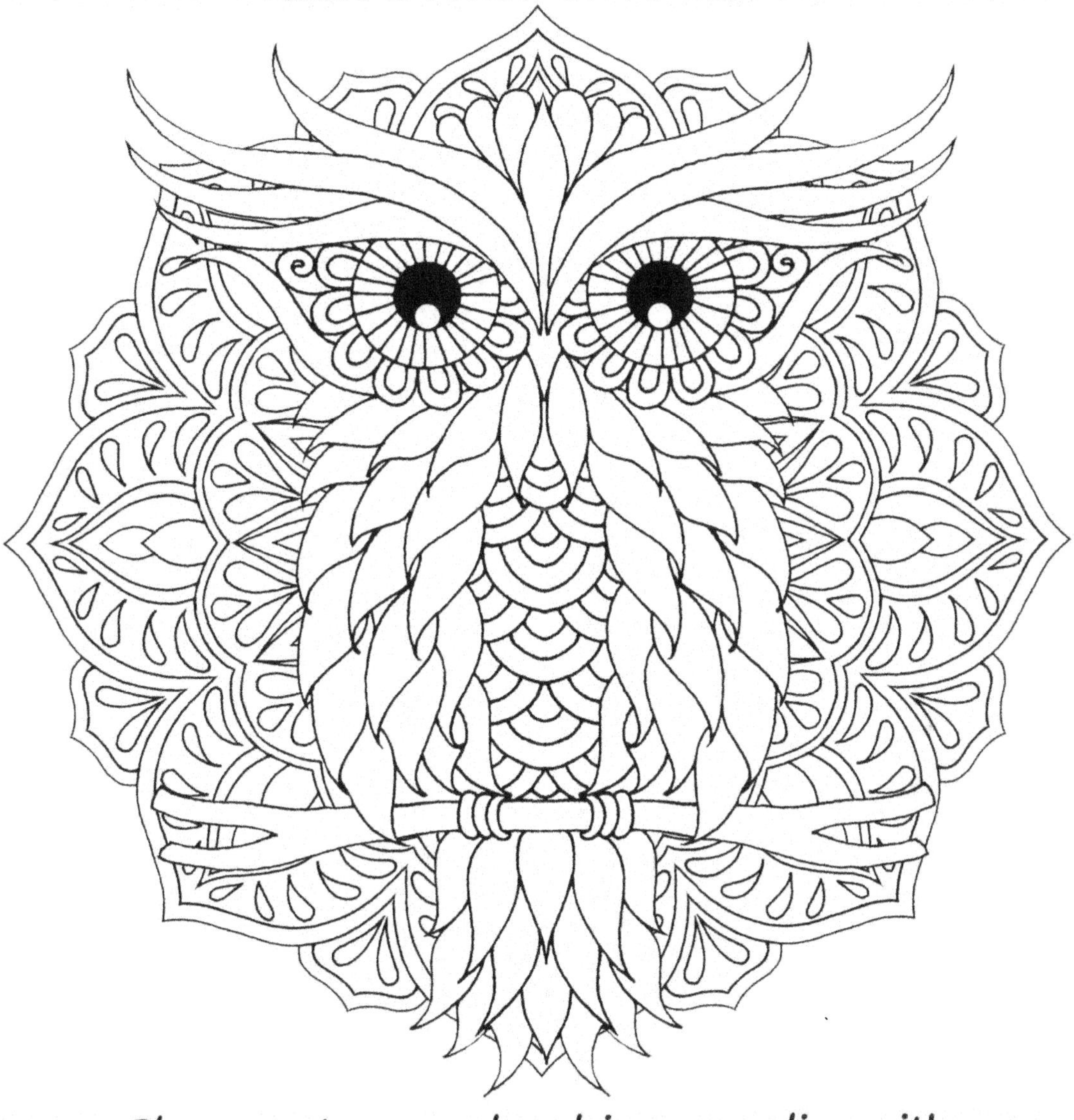

Please post your colored images online with
#tabbystangledart or **#tabbyb** so I can find them easily.

Instagram: @tabbystangledart
Twitter: @tabbyleann
www.patreon.com/tabbyb
www.sellfy.com/tabbyb
www.redbubble.com/people/tabbyb
www.amazon.com/author/tabbystangledart
http://tinyurl.com/tabbytube

www.ingramcontent.com/pod-product-compliance
Lightning Source LLC
Chambersburg PA
CBHW082333220526
45470CB00008B/2496
* 9 7 8 1 9 7 5 9 1 7 4 4 9 *